P9-DMQ-952

Emeril's

THERE'S A CHEF
IN MY SOUP!

Recipes for the Kid in Everyone

Emeril's

THERE'S A CHEF IN MY SOUP!

Recipes for the Kid in Everyone

by EMERIL LAGASSE

VENS MEMORIAL LIBRARY
Memorial Drive
ham, MA 01400
978-827-4115
Fax 978-827-4116

Illustrated by Charles Yuen

 HarperCollinsPublishers

For information on Emeril Lagasse or his books
and products, please contact:
Emeril's Homebase
829 St. Charles Avenue
New Orleans, Louisiana 70130
Tel: (800) 980–8474
(504) 558–3940
www.emerils.com

Emeril's There's a Chef in My Soup!
Interior photos of Emeril by Quentin Bacon
All illustrations, drawings, photography, text, and recipes are the property of Emeril's
Food of Love Productions LLC, used by permission. © 2002 Emeril's Food of Love
Productions LLC.
Printed in the U.S.A. All rights reserved.
www.harperchildrens.com

Library of Congress Cataloging-in-Publication Data
Lagasse, Emeril.
  [There's a chef in my soup!]
  Emeril's there's a chef in my soup! : recipes for the kid in everyone / by Emeril
Lagasse ; illustrated by Charles Yuen ; photography by Quentin Bacon.
    p.   cm.
  Summary: World-famous chef Emeril Lagasse shares some of his favorite recipes
that children can make, as well as tips for the whole family on how to have fun and
be safe in the kitchen.
  ISBN 0-688-17706-9
  1. Cookery—Juvenile literature. [1. Cookery.] I. Title: Emeril's there's a chef in my
soup!
II. Yuen, Charles, ill. III. Bacon, Quentin, ill. IV. Title.
TX652.5 .L33 2002   2001039678
641.5—dc21   CIP
                                                               AC

Design by Charles Yuen

Endpaper drawings courtesy of Hannah Alford, Madi Alford, Jada Brooks, Nicholas
Halphen, Trevor Laborde, Lauren Linquest, Megan Linquest, Bronson Lott, Landon
Lott, Logan Lott, Annie McGrew, Evelyn Martinson, Kelsey Reese, and Neil Ripley

1 2 3 4 5 6 7 8 9 10

❖

First Edition

To Jessica and Jillian Lagasse,
my sweet daughters—
May you have a happy-happy life

&

To my young fans and friends for
whom this book was written—
May cooking always be a great
source of joy and inspiration!

ALSO BY EMERIL LAGASSE

Prime Time Emeril
(2001)

Emeril's New New Orleans Cooking
with Jessie Tirsch (1993)

Louisiana Real & Rustic
with Marcelle Bienvenu (1996)

Emeril's Creole Christmas
with Marcelle Bienvenu (1997)

Emeril's TV Dinners
with Marcelle Bienvenu and Felicia Willett (1998)

Every Day's a Party
with Marcelle Bienvenu and Felicia Willett (1999)

ACKNOWLEDGMENTS

A lot of love has gone into the making of this book, and I would like to thank the following people for helping THERE'S A CHEF IN MY SOUP! come to life:

- Miss Hilda and Mr. John, my mom and dad, for sharing your love of food with me from an early age

- My sweet wife, Alden, for your constant love and support in everything that I do

- Charlotte Armstrong, who had an incredible vision and a terrific feel with kids, not to mention an amazing culinary talent. I thank you from the bottom of my heart.

- My awesome Culinary Team at Homebase— Chef David McCelvey, Marcelle Bienvenu, Charlotte Armstrong, Trevor Wisdom, and Alain Joseph, for keeping me on track

- All the Homebase parents and kids who turned out for the children's art party, especially Hannah Alford, Madi Alford, Jada Brooks, Nicholas Halphen, Trevor Laborde, Lauren Linquest, Megan Linquest, Bronson Lott, Landon Lott, Logan Lott, Evelyn Martinson, Annie McGrew, Kelsey Reese, and Neil Ripley—your artwork rules!

- Beth Lott and Helen Lansden, for helping with the children's art party

- Marti Dalton and Mara Warner, for orchestrating my life!

- My loyal fans and tough critics whose quotes appear on the back of this book: Jada Brooks, Mallory Cruz, Nicholas Halphen, Susannah Lawrence, Megan Linquest, Annie McGrew, and Neil Ripley

- Mallory Cruz and Lauren Linquest, for sharing your delicious recipes with me

- My compadres in all things, Eric Linquest, Tony Cruz, and Mauricio Andrade

- All the folks at Emeril's Homebase, Emeril's Restaurant, NOLA, and Emeril's Delmonico Restaurant in New Orleans; Emeril's New Orleans Fish House and Delmonico Steakhouse in Las Vegas; and Emeril's Restaurant Orlando, for making me proud to be part of such an incredible team

- Photographers Quentin Bacon, David Langley, and Kerri McCaffety

- All the folks at HarperCollins Children's Books who shared the vision with me:

  Susan Katz, Publisher; Kate Jackson, Senior V.P., Associate Publisher, and Editor-in-Chief; Toni Markiet, Executive Editor; Harriett Barton, V.P., Creative Director; Robin Stamm, Associate Editor; Carrie Klusacek, Editorial Assistant; Fumi Kosaka, Design Assistant; Pam Lutz, V.P., Director of Marketing; Mary McAveney, Director of Hardcover Marketing; Allison Devlin, Executive Director of Publicity; Carrie Weinberg, Director of Publicity (Adult Division); Lucille Schneider, Associate Director of Production; Laurie Kahn, Senior Production Editor; Emma Jackson, Brandon Harris, and Alex Yuen

- And lastly but not leastly, to Charles Yuen, whose out-of-this-world illustrations capture the spirit of these recipes!

Emeril's
THERE'S A CHEF IN MY SOUP!

Recipes for the Kid in Everyone

CONTENTS

"P" Is for Pizza and Pasta

What's for Lunch?

THE MAIN THING

EAT YOUR VEGGIES!

CONTENTS

Emeril's

THERE'S A CHEF
IN MY SOUP!

Recipes for the Kid in Everyone

My friends! I'm so happy to see so many of you cooking these days. You know why? Because cooking is really fun, fun, fun, and it makes people happy, happy, happy!

When I was a little boy, I used to watch my mom, Miss Hilda, cook. I saw how people loved to come to our house to eat her food, and I decided cooking was something I wanted to be able to do, too. I watched everything she did, and she let me help in the kitchen. Little by little, I began cooking by myself. I started with simple stuff, like vegetable soup and French toast. At first, things like chopping and whisking were kind of hard. My chopped veggies were all different sizes and my whisked sauces were all over the floor! But hey—I kept on, and the more I did these things, the better I got. When I was a teenager I got my first job—in a bakery. I learned how to make things like pizza and pretzels and, boy, was I making people happy with those! The more I cooked, the happier people got. Best of all, I was enjoying myself doing it. Now you know why I decided to become a chef.

I really had no idea how many friends I would make just by cooking—friends like you. I also had no idea at first how many kids wanted to cook for themselves, but I soon found out. So, not too long ago, I said to myself, "Self, why not write a special cookbook for all of my young friends and fans out there?" So here it is! THERE'S A CHEF IN MY SOUP! was written with you in mind. It has the kind of foods that kids of all ages can make and enjoy eating—things like Gooey Cinnamon Buns, Tuna Melts in Your Mouth, My-Oh-My Spaghetti Pie, Shake-It-Up-a-Notch Chicken, Baby Bam Burgers, Pokey Brownies—you name it! There are some really easy recipes for beginners, like

HEY, KIDS— LISTEN UP!

Yummy Wake-Up Smoothies or Emeril's First Alphabet Soup. For those of you with more experience, there are some tougher recipes, too, such as Twist Yourself a Pretzel or Gingerbread Friends. There are lots of recipes to choose from—seventy-five in all—pick the ones that sound good to you!

But before you start cooking, do me a favor and remember the following things:

ASK PERMISSION!

Remember to ask your parents' permission before you begin to cook. Hey, why not let them be your helper in the kitchen? You will learn things together, and the best part is this: At the end, you will have something yummy to enjoy together as a family.

BE SAFE!

Before getting started, make sure you read about how to be safe in the kitchen on pages 8–11. This is really important!

BE PREPARED!

Cook like the pros do. Read through the recipe you want to make and look up any words or techniques you don't know on pages 18–28. And gather together everything you need—both ingredients and tools—before you start cooking. It makes cooking a snap.

BE CLEAN!

Cleaning is a big part of cooking. Your food needs to be safe and healthy and, if you clean as you go along, when you're ready to sit down and enjoy what you've cooked, you won't have mountains of dishes to worry about.

HAVE FUN!

Most of all, remember to enjoy your time in the kitchen and learn to do things your way. Experiment and make changes that work for you.

So, let's go—get in the kitchen and get cooking! Have fun, be careful, experiment, and share your creations with your family and friends. And remember, it's a "food of love" thing. . . .

BAM!

Chef Emeril

Some of my very best childhood memories revolve around food and being in the kitchen with my family and friends. My mom, Miss Hilda, has always been an awesome cook, and she lovingly shared her time and her kitchen with me when I was younger. Our kitchen was the center of our family life together. I saw firsthand the joy that food could inspire in people, and these memories are still with me today. Because of this, I've never lost sight of the importance of time spent preparing and enjoying food together.

For a while, I'd begun to think that this ideal was a thing of the past. I know that a lot of families are so busy with work and sports and classes and meetings and everything else that there is no time to eat together, let alone cook together! But lately I've become optimistic about the future. With the passing of each year, I've seen more and more young people interested in food and cooking. As a matter of fact, many of my most loyal fans are children. That is my real reason for wanting to write THERE'S A CHEF IN MY SOUP!

I know from my shows and the letters I get that there are kids out there who are *really cooking*! They take turns preparing

4

breakfast or school lunches. They're even making some pretty kicked-up suppers. I think this is terrific! Cooking together is not only a great way for the whole family to share the responsibility of mealtimes, but it's also a lot of fun. And best of all, it's a great way for kids (and you, too) to be creative. Now is an exciting time for kids to discover cooking—the past twenty years have really changed the way the world looks at food. Restaurants and grocery stores that showcase food from all over the world are everywhere. TV is full of excellent chefs who show you how to make delicious food and how to choose and use all the best ingredients. Food doesn't just fill our bellies anymore, it fills all our senses, and cooking isn't a chore, it's an art form. I truly believe that kids understand this in a very fundamental way. The possibilities for creative expression are endless. So hey—even if you're not much of a cook yourself, why not learn the tools and techniques of the trade along with your children? I know you'll both enjoy the time spent together—and having fun together is the key to this whole thing.

And don't forget the added bonus of how much there is to be learned in the kitchen! By simply learning to follow a recipe, we practice reading and organizational skills. Math skills are key in learning to measure ingredients. Since cooking is all about chemistry, we even get to learn a little science. The habits you learn in the kitchen—safety, cleanliness,

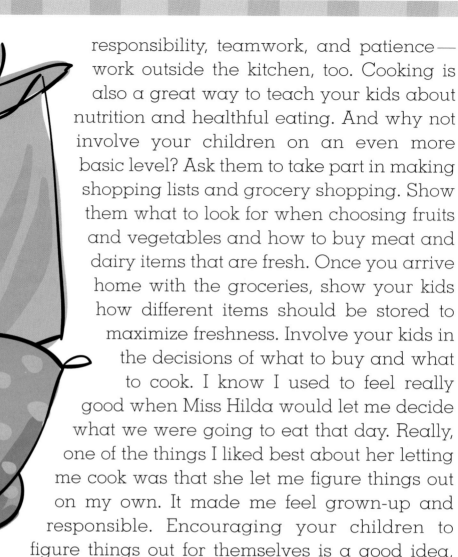

responsibility, teamwork, and patience—work outside the kitchen, too. Cooking is also a great way to teach your kids about nutrition and healthful eating. And why not involve your children on an even more basic level? Ask them to take part in making shopping lists and grocery shopping. Show them what to look for when choosing fruits and vegetables and how to buy meat and dairy items that are fresh. Once you arrive home with the groceries, show your kids how different items should be stored to maximize freshness. Involve your kids in the decisions of what to buy and what to cook. I know I used to feel really good when Miss Hilda would let me decide what we were going to eat that day. Really, one of the things I liked best about her letting me cook was that she let me figure things out on my own. It made me feel grown-up and responsible. Encouraging your children to figure things out for themselves is a good idea, as long as you're available for help and guidance along the way.

Now, don't be afraid to let your kids work in the kitchen. Just make sure you know what they're doing at all times and that you're there to help them if and when they need it. I've seen time and time again that accidents are most likely to happen when anyone who works in the kitchen, at any age, isn't aware of the most basic hows and whys of being safe. I've included a lot of tips on being safe in the kitchen on pages 8–11. I've tried to present them in a language that is not frightening but still lets the kids know it's really important to follow them. Please take the time to read the safety section with your kids and talk about how to be safe in the kitchen. If you do that, there's no reason for you or your kids to be afraid of cooking and using kitchen tools with care.

If you and your children haven't spent much time together in the kitchen so far, don't panic! It doesn't have to be a scary thing—just remember to be with your child in the kitchen in a way that feels right for you. If you're more comfortable with formalities, so be it—set the table, break out the linens, and teach your child about proper dining etiquette. Design a menu together from soup to nuts, and then enjoy a three- or four-course dinner. If you're a more relaxed kind of family, you might prefer to sit around the kitchen together sharing a Big-Boy Pizza or digging into bowls of Some Real Good Chili. You want to use paper plates and napkins? Go ahead! Do it your way. Or hey—try both ways!

In the end, the most important thing is that your kids have had fun, they've created something all their own, and you've spent time together as a family. If you happen to learn something new along the way, too, well, that's just the cherry on top! Cook together, eat together, and be together— you'll give your child the real gift of memories that will be with them always.

A GOOD COOK IS A SAFE COOK!

Hey, cooking is a lot of fun! I love everything about working in the kitchen—how the food looks, feels, and smells and of course how it tastes when you're all done. But it's really important to remember that cooking is serious stuff. If you don't pay attention in the kitchen, you can get hurt very easily—and I want to be sure that doesn't happen. So before we get started, let's go over some ways to be safe in the kitchen.

ASK FOR HELP!

- Remember to *always* ask permission from your mom or dad or any adult in charge before you begin cooking.

- Never cook by yourself. It's always a good idea to have an adult nearby, especially when using sharp knives or graters, electrical appliances, hot burners, and the oven.

- You can do a lot of things yourself if you're careful, but ask for help when you need it—like lifting heavy pots. Being smart in the kitchen is important!

- You have to dress right for the kitchen—not to look good but to be safe and comfortable. Cooking clothes should be roomy but not too loose. Loose clothing can get caught on equipment, and you always have to be especially careful around an open flame. Long sleeves should be rolled up tight so they don't get in the way.

- Loose, long hair is a big no-no! If you have long hair, tie it back so it doesn't get in your way or into the food.

- Most jewelry isn't safe in the kitchen. Don't wear anything that dangles. If you wear a watch, be sure it's waterproof.

BE PREPARED!

- Always review the recipe you will be preparing before you begin. Make sure you have all the ingredients you need, and that all the tools and equipment are ready. Believe it or not, I still do this.

8

- If you don't understand how to do something, ask an adult to explain it to you before you begin cooking.

- I like to measure out all my ingredients before I start. I cut, chop, mince, and mix ahead when I can, too. It makes cooking a breeze.

BE CLEAN!

- Cleanliness is very important in the kitchen. I know I sound like a grown-up but it's really true. You want the food you serve to be healthy and safe.

- Make sure you wash your hands especially well before and after handling raw meat—particularly poultry (chicken, duck, and raw eggs). Raw poultry can carry a germ called salmonella, which can make you very sick.

- Here's a big secret we professional chefs have that I'll let you in on: It's a smart idea to clean up as you go along. That way, any tools that you need again will be clean and ready for you, and you'll have plenty of room on your counter to work. Best of all, you won't end up with a mountain of dirty dishes just when you want to be sitting down to enjoy your yummy creation.

- Never put knives or other sharp objects in sinks filled with water and other utensils—you can cut yourself when you reach into the water. It also damages the blades. It's best when working with knives to wash them well with soap and water as soon as you're finished with them.

- Cutting boards should always be washed with soap and warm water after each use. When you're using them to prepare raw meat or poultry, you have to be even more careful than usual! Unclean cutting boards can pass germs along to other foods, and some germs (like salmonella) can make you sick. When in doubt wash, wash, wash.

STAY COOL WHEN COOKING WITH FIRE!

- It's really important to have an adult close by whenever you're cooking on the stove or in the oven, and they should be around from start to finish, when you turn the appliance off. Don't ever use the stove—or the oven—when you're home alone!

- Be extra careful of hot surfaces when cooking. It's easy to tell when a stovetop with a gas (open) flame is on; it's less obvious on stoves with electric or radiant burners, which are just as hot. Check your stovetop or oven controls carefully before you get to work.

- Pot holders and oven mitts rule in the kitchen! If you're not sure if something is hot, use pot holders or mitts just to be on the safe side. And hey—it's really important that pot holders and oven mitts are dry when you use them. If they're wet, the heat will go right through them and burn you faster than you can say, "Bam!"

- Never, ever leave food unattended while it's cooking!

- Always remember that the outside surface of the oven also gets hot when the oven is on, so don't lean against it when it's on.

- When cooking on top of the stove, always remember to turn your long pot handles to the side or toward the center. But make sure they're not over an open flame. They shouldn't hang over the edge of the stove, either—someone might walk by and knock into them by accident.

- Keep as far away as possible from hot, bubbling liquids. The bubbles can pop and splatter, and that can really burn. It's also a good idea to use long-handled wooden spoons to stir hot things.

- When moving heavy pots filled with hot liquids or when lifting heavy roasting pans out of the oven, you need to be smart. If you're sure you can do it, use pot holders and be really careful. If you even think for a minute that the pot or pan is too heavy for you, don't try to do it yourself. Ask an adult to help you!

- Remember to always uncover a hot pot so that the side of the lid farthest away from you tilts up first. This way the steam will be as far away from you as possible. Steam burns can really hurt! The same thing goes for draining a pot that is full of hot liquid—always pour out, *away* from you, so that the liquid and steam do not burn your hands or your face.

- If you do happen to burn or cut yourself, or in case of a fire, call an adult *immediately*!

KNOW YOUR TOOLS AND BE PATIENT!

- Kitchen tools are just like any other tools—you have to know how to use them the right way. This is for your safety and also to help you take care of your tools. If you're not familiar with the right way to hold and use knives or other equipment, ask your mom or dad or the supervising adult to show you, or check out our techniques section (pages 18–28) for the right ways to use most kitchen equipment.

- When learning how to work in the kitchen, be patient. It's better to practice any technique slowly—particularly chopping, slicing, or mincing. That way you can be precise and safe. You will be surprised to see that with just a little practice, you'll become good at it in no time.

- Watch out using graters—they're as sharp as knives! It's real easy to scrape fingers and knuckles when you're not paying attention.

- You have to be really careful when using electrical appliances such as the toaster, microwave oven, toaster oven, blenders, and mixers. These are powerful tools that should be used with caution. Here are some quick tips to follow at all times:

— Always be sure your hands are dry when you plug something in.

— Never, ever put your hands or fingers inside any electrical appliance when it's on.

— Remember to pull your hair back and not wear dangling jewelry.

— Hey, make sure the lid on your blender is on tight—if it's not, your food will go all over the kitchen instead of inside your mouth.

— Always turn your mixer **off** before scraping down the sides of the bowl or adding ingredients. If a spoon or spatula gets caught in the turning beaters, you'll ruin the mixer and maybe hurt yourself, too.

— When you turn the mixer back on after adding ingredients, start on the slowest speed. That way, your ingredients won't splash all over you.

CAUTION

To help you stay safe, we've included little safety icons. You and your folks will know with one quick look how careful you'll need to be. Here's what they are and what they mean:

 This recipe requires adult supervision. With the exception of easy sandwiches, which don't require the use of sharp objects, heat, or electrical appliances, this symbol will be on almost all the recipes.

This recipe requires the use of sharp objects such as knives or graters. You need an adult around to help, and you need to pay attention!

 This recipe requires the use of electrical appliances.

 This recipe requires cooking either on the stovetop or in the oven. You have to be very, very careful and have an adult in the kitchen.

 This recipe requires handling hot objects from either the stovetop or the oven. Be sure to use oven mitts or pot holders!

THE NUTS AND BOLTS

Here are some of the tools you'll use most often in the kitchen.

1. KNIVES

chef's knife

bread knife
(serrated edge)

paring knife

butter knife

2. CUTTING BOARDS

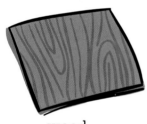

wood

plastic

3. MIXING BOWLS

metal

glass

plastic

NOTE: Plastic or glass bowls should always be used when a recipe calls for a nonreactive bowl. Metal "reacts" with acidic foods such as vinegar and lemon juice, and this makes the food taste funny.

4. SPOONS

wooden   metal   serving

5. COLANDERS

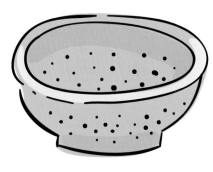

plastic   metal

6. STRAINERS

coarse mesh   fine mesh   sieve   sifter

7. MEASURING CUPS

glass   plastic   metal

8. MEASURING SPOONS

plastic   metal

9. WHISK

10. SPATULAS AND TURNERS

rubber spatula   metal turner   plastic turner   wood turner

NOTE: Always use plastic or wood for nonstick pans so you don't damage their surface.

11. TONGS

plastic   metal

12. LADLE

13. VEGETABLE PEELER

14. VEGETABLE BRUSH

15. GRATERS

multiple-sided   single-sided

16. ZESTER

14

17. POTATO MASHERS

18. GARLIC PRESS

19. APPLE CORER

20. PASTRY BRUSH

21. SKEWERS

metal   bamboo

NOTE: Always soak bamboo skewers in water for 30 minutes before using.

22. INSTANT-READ THERMOMETER

23. OVEN MITTS AND POT HOLDERS

24. ROLLING PIN

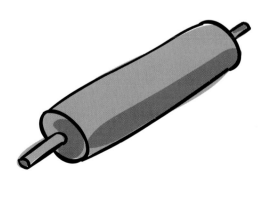

25. KITCHEN TIMER

26. MIXERS

handheld   standing electric

27. BLENDER

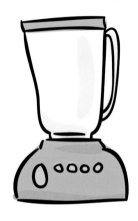

28. WIRE RACK

29. SALAD SPINNER

30. SALAD TOSSERS

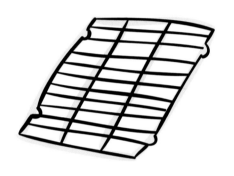

31. POTS AND PANS

  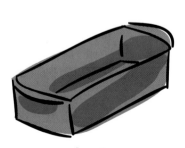

skillet   saucepan   loaf pan

muffin pan

baking sheet

springform pan

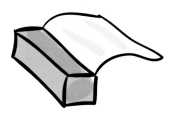

baking dish

Dutch oven

cast-iron corn stick pan

32. COOKING AIDS

paper muffin-tin liners

plastic wrap

parchment paper

aluminum foil

33. DOUBLE BOILER

LET'S GET STARTED

Good Things to Know

WASHING Fresh veggies and fruits should always be rinsed well under cold running water and then patted dry with paper towels before using. Some veggies, such as potatoes, need to be scrubbed well with a vegetable brush. Meat, poultry, and seafood should be washed before using, too. Simply rinse under cold water and then pat dry with paper towels before continuing.

PEELING Some fruits and veggies peel easily with a vegetable peeler. Place the food (such as a carrot, cucumber, potato, apple, or pear) on a cutting board and hold firmly with one hand. Using the other hand, scrape the peeler down the length of the food. Keep turning as you go, so that you remove all of the peel.

Other foods, such as onions and garlic, are peeled differently. Use a sharp knife to cut a little off of both ends. Then use your fingers to peel away the dry, tough outer layers. For garlic, press down on it with the palm of your hand to loosen the skin. It will then peel off very easily.

CHOPPING When chopping round foods like potatoes or carrots, the first thing you should do is cut off a small piece from one side so that it doesn't roll away while you're cutting it. Place this flat part down on the cutting board. Then, hold one side of the food firmly with one hand and cut the food to the shape or size desired. The more you chop, the smaller the pieces will get.

ROUGHLY CHOPPED

FINELY CHOPPED

MINCED

When it comes to chopping, onions are in a league all their own! Once they're peeled, cut them in half lengthwise and place them flat side down on the cutting board. Then, while holding the root end with your fingers, make many

lengthwise cuts all the way down to the cutting board. Then turn your knife and cut across the lengthwise cuts. Pieces of onion will fall away on the cutting board. The closer your cuts are to one another, the smaller the pieces of onion will be!

Mincing garlic is easy! Separate the head of garlic into cloves. Peel as described on page 18, then use your chef's knife or a paring knife to cut the

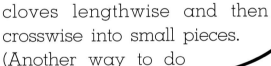

cloves lengthwise and then crosswise into small pieces. (Another way to do this is with a garlic press, which is really easy and safe—and fun! Just put the garlic into the press, close it, and press real hard. Little pieces of garlic—just the right size—will come out of the holes!)

GRATING When grating hard foods, like carrots or potatoes, hold the grater with one hand and the piece of food firmly in the other. Rub the end of the veggie downward over the holes, back and forth over a large mixing bowl or piece of waxed paper, and the grated pieces will fall through the holes. Be very careful not to grate your fingers—that hurts! Soft foods, such as cheese, are really easy to grate!

CORING APPLES

- **WITH AN APPLE CORER:** Hold the apple firmly on your cutting board. Center the apple corer over the core and press down firmly until you feel the corer hit the cutting board. Twist and pull corer out of the apple, and the core should come right out.

- **WITH A PARING KNIFE:** Cut the apple in half. Cut each half in half again. Place the apple on the cutting board and cut the core away from the apple.

- **WITH A MELON BALLER:** This is the easiest way to core an apple! Cut an apple in half. Place the apple half on the cutting board, core side up. Hold the melon baller in your other hand and center it over the core of the apple. Press down into the apple and twist. A round piece of apple core should come right out.

HULLING STRAWBERRIES Place the strawberry on the cutting board and hold the pointed side with one hand. Using a paring knife, cut across the top to remove the stem.

FRUITS WITH PITS (SUCH AS PEACHES, NECTARINES, CHERRIES, PLUMS) To remove the pit, simply cut the fruit in half along the indentation, then twist the two halves apart.

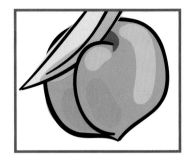

ZESTING You can "zest" any citrus fruit (lemons, limes, oranges, or grapefruits). Using a "zester," it's really easy. Simply pull the zester down the side of a piece of fruit, pressing at the same time so that the zester removes tiny strips of the outermost layer of peel. If you don't have a zester, a fine grater works too. Over a bowl or a piece of waxed paper, rub the side of the fruit along the grater while lightly pressing down. The small pieces of zest will fall through the grater. Be sure you get only the colored part of the peel: The white part is bitter!

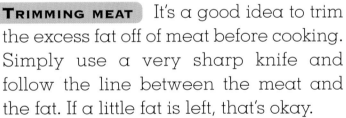

TRIMMING MEAT It's a good idea to trim the excess fat off of meat before cooking. Simply use a very sharp knife and follow the line between the meat and the fat. If a little fat is left, that's okay.

CRACKING AND SEPARATING EGGS To crack an egg, hold it firmly in one hand while you hit the middle part (not too hard!) against the rim of a bowl. Then take both hands and grasp the cracked edges and pull apart. It's always a good idea to crack an egg into a separate bowl before adding it to a recipe so that you can see if any bits of shell fell into the egg. (If so, remove them before adding the egg to the recipe!) Sometimes a recipe will call for just egg yolks or egg whites. To separate eggs and use either the yolk or white only, crack

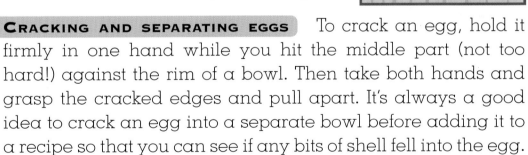

the egg lightly and pull the halves apart, carefully letting the white drip into a cup. Keep the yolk in the eggshell. Gently move the yolk from one eggshell half to the other, letting the white drip into the cup until only the yolk is left in the shell. Be careful not to break the yolk so that it bleeds into the egg white.

CUTTING CHICKENS If a recipe calls for a whole chicken cut into pieces, please don't try to cut one up yourself. This is really hard and very dangerous. Either have your parents do it for you or buy a cut-up chicken at the grocery store.

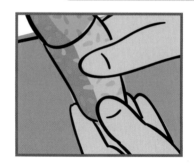

REMOVING SAUSAGE FROM CASING Sometimes sausage comes stuffed in "casing," which keeps it together. To remove the sausage from the casing, simply use the point of a sharp knife to cut the tip off of one end of the sausage link and squeeze from the bottom up to force the meat mixture out.

HOW TO KNOW WHEN ENOUGH IS ENOUGH

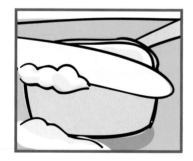

MEASURING It's best to use individual ¼-, ⅓-, ½-, and 1-cup measuring cups when you can—it's the easiest and most accurate way to measure things. When measuring dry ingredients such as flour, sugar, or rice, use a metal or plastic measuring cup like that shown above. Dip the appropriate size measuring cup into the ingredient that is to be measured, then use a knife or your hand to level off the top.

When measuring liquids, use glass or plastic measuring cups that you can see through. Fill until the liquid comes to the appropriate line on the cup, checking at eye level to make sure you've measured the correct amount.

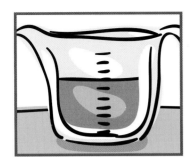

Measuring spoons are easy to use. For dry foods, just dip the spoons into whatever you're measuring, then level off the top. For liquids, such as oil or vanilla extract, hold the spoon in one hand and pour with the other. Make sure to hold the spoon level, and always fill it all the way to the top!

DETERMINING CONTAINER CAPACITY If you're not sure of the size of a saucepan, baking dish, or other container, simply use a measuring cup to fill it with water. Count the number of cups it takes to fill the container and then figure out its size by referring to the equivalents chart on page 28.

NOW WE'RE COOKING!

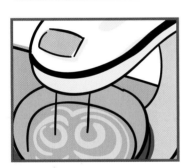

MIXING Just another term for combining things, usually with a "mixer," which has beaters instead of spoons. Lock the beaters into the mixer, lower the beaters into the mixing bowl, then turn the power on slowly. As the mixture becomes more blended, you can increase the speed.

BEATING This means mixing things together quickly so that air is added to the mixture and it becomes smooth and creamy. Usually done with a mixer, you can also beat things with a spoon—it just takes a little elbow grease!

STIRRING Use a spoon to stir in a circular motion until the ingredients are all blended.

FOLDING This is a way of mixing things together very gently so that they stay fluffy. Use a large plastic or rubber spatula and, instead of stirring, place it into the bowl and combine the ingredients with two or three up-and-over, or "folding," motions. Don't overmix!

SIFTING This is done to make sure there are no lumps in dry foods like flour or sugar. Just hold the sifter over a bowl and shake from side to side (some sifters have knobs to turn or handles to squeeze).

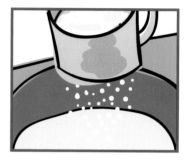

CREAMING This refers to beating butter and sugar together very well until it becomes light and "creamy."

SOFT PEAKS This term is used when beating things like heavy cream or egg whites. After you turn the mixer off and lift the beaters out of the bowl, if a little of the mixture comes up where the beaters were, forming a soft mound that stays up, that's a soft peak.

SCRAPING DOWN BOWL This is done to make sure everything gets mixed evenly. Just hold the edge of the mixing bowl in one hand, then run a plastic or rubber spatula all the way around the inside of the bowl to "scrape down" the sides.

EGGS Eggs come in different sizes. When using eggs for the recipes in this book, always use the ones labeled LARGE.

WORKING BUTTER INTO FLOUR You can do this with a pastry blender, two forks or butter knives, or your fingers. The main thing is that the butter is rubbed into the flour so that only small pieces of butter are visible and the rest has been combined with the flour. When it's done, it will look like small crumbs.

SOFTENING BUTTER If a recipe calls for butter to be softened, it means at room temperature—not straight from the refrigerator. If you forget to take the butter out to soften, try placing it in a microwave-proof bowl and microwave on high for 5 to 10 seconds. This works great.

ROLLING DOUGH Place the dough on a lightly floured surface and sprinkle the top with flour. Using a rolling pin, roll while pressing down on the dough. Begin by rolling front to back, then switch directions and roll side to side. If the rolling pin sticks, sprinkle a little more flour. Continue rolling until the dough is the desired size and thickness.

GREASING A PAN Greasing helps keep baked goods from sticking to the pan. It's easy to do this with your hands, but if you don't want to get stuff all over them, then try using a paper towel to spread the shortening or oil. Just make sure you don't miss any spots!

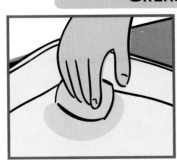

MEASURING THICKNESS OF DOUGH Until you have a lot of practice with this, it's a good idea to keep a ruler handy. This is an easy way to see if you've rolled your dough out to the correct thickness.

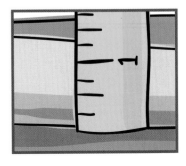

KNEADING DOUGH Place the dough on a lightly floured surface. Use one hand to firmly press into one side of the dough. Pick up the other side of the dough with your other hand and fold it over, again pressing into the dough. Pick up the opposite edge of the dough

and do the same. Repeat this process for as long as instructed in the individual recipe directions. The dough should become smooth and elastic. If the dough gets sticky, sprinkle with a bit more flour.

PROOFING YEAST This is a way of making sure the yeast is working! Let it sit for about 5 minutes in a warm liquid. If it's working, you will see lots of foam and little bubbles rise to the surface.

MELTING CHOCOLATE IN A DOUBLE BOILER Fill the bottom of a double boiler with about 2 inches of water. Insert the top of the double boiler and place the chocolate in it. Set on the stovetop and simmer on low heat, stirring occasionally until the chocolate is melted. If you don't have a double boiler, you can use a medium saucepan for the bottom part and a metal bowl large enough to sit on top of the saucepan without touching the water at the bottom.

IS IT DONE YET?

TESTING THE HEAT OF A PAN
You can test the heat of a pan by dropping a teaspoon of water in it. The pan is hot enough to cook in when the water "dances" into drops across the bottom.

TESTING WITH TOOTHPICKS This is an easy trick! Insert a toothpick into the center of a cake—if it comes out clean when you pull it out, the cake is done. If you can see gooey stuff or bits of crumbs sticking to it, then it needs a bit more cooking time.

THERMOMETER USAGE Some recipes in this book suggest using an instant-read thermometer when things need to be at a certain temperature. Though this is not always necessary, a thermometer does help you make sure that things are cooked enough. Thermometers also help when cooking with yeast, because you usually need to add warm water or other liquid to it in order for it to start working. A thermometer will tell you if the liquid is too hot or too cold. (If you use a thermometer, make sure that it is inserted far enough into whatever you're testing so that you get a true temperature.)

FORK-TENDER When you insert a fork into something and it goes in easily, then it is said to be fork-tender.

MEAT DONENESS Because some meat may contain germs that can make you sick, it's a good idea to cook your meat until it's no longer pink inside. This is called being "cooked through." Even better, if you have an instant-read thermometer, simply insert the tip into the meat (there is usually a mark on the thermometer that shows how far it should be inserted), wait a few seconds until the temperature stops rising, and then read the number. For beef, medium well to well done is 150° to 165°F. For chicken, turkey, or pork, always cook to at least 160°F.

KICK UP THE FLAVOR!

DRIED VS. FRESH HERBS Most of the recipes in this book call for dried herbs, since this is what most folks have at home. It's really easy to kick them up a notch by rubbing them between your fingers before adding them to the recipe. They will release more flavor this way! And hey, if your mom or dad has an herb garden and you have access to fresh herbs, feel free to use them in recipes. Just take the leaves off of the stems and chop into small pieces with a knife. Remember, though, that to get the same amount of flavor from fresh herbs, you'll have to use about 3 times the amount of dried herbs called for in the recipe.

PEPPER When a recipe calls for ground black pepper, the kind you buy in spice jars or tins is just fine. However, if you have a pepper mill at home, there's nothing like the flavor of fresh-ground pepper.

Measurement Equivalents

3 TEASPOONS = 1 TABLESPOON

4 TABLESPOONS = ¼ CUP

1 CUP = ½ PINT = 8 OUNCES

2 CUPS = 1 PINT = 16 OUNCES

2 PINTS = 1 QUART = 32 OUNCES

4 QUARTS = 1 GALLON = 128 OUNCES

1 STICK BUTTER = 8 TABLESPOONS = ¼ POUND = ½ CUP

Emeril's
THERE'S A CHEF IN MY SOUP!
Recipes for the Kid in Everyone

FIRST THINGS FIRST!

CHAPTER 1

Emeril's Favorite French Toast

Yield

4 TO 8 SERVINGS

Ingredients

4 LARGE EGGS

1 CUP WHOLE MILK

¼ CUP FRESHLY SQUEEZED ORANGE JUICE

1 TABLESPOON ORANGE ZEST (PAGE 21)

2 TEASPOONS GRANULATED SUGAR

½ TEASPOON VANILLA EXTRACT

⅛ TEASPOON SALT

8 SLICES BREAD

8 TEASPOONS UNSALTED BUTTER

CONFECTIONERS' SUGAR

MAPLE SYRUP OR CANE SUGAR (OPTIONAL)

Tools

MEASURING CUPS AND SPOONS, ORANGE ZESTER OR FINE GRATER, LARGE MIXING BOWL, WIRE WHISK, PLATE, 6-INCH NONSTICK SKILLET, PLASTIC TURNER, BAKING SHEET, ALUMINUM FOIL, OVEN MITTS OR POT HOLDERS

Oh, man, talk about a walk down memory lane. This is one of the first things I ever made in the kitchen when I was a little boy. Even back then I liked to experiment to keep things interesting, and this is the result of one very successful experiment. The orange flavor in this French toast will just about knock your socks off. Try it—I bet you'll be back for more!

Directions

CAUTION

1 Preheat the oven to 200°F.

2 Crack the eggs into a large mixing bowl and whisk well.

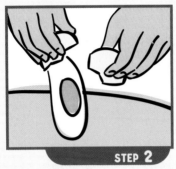
STEP 2

3 Add the milk, orange juice, orange zest, granulated sugar, vanilla extract, and salt, and whisk until well combined.

4 Working quickly, dip each bread slice into the egg mixture in the bowl, turning it to coat both sides with the mixture. Transfer the coated bread slices to a plate while you finish coating the remaining slices.

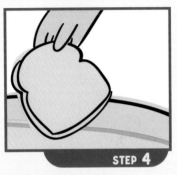
STEP 4

5 Heat a small skillet over medium heat until hot, about 3 to 5 minutes.

6 Melt 1 teaspoon of the butter in the skillet, then add a slice of coated bread, and cook until the bread is golden brown and crusted on the bottom, about 2 minutes. Turn with a plastic turner and cook until the second side is golden, about 1 to 1½ minutes.

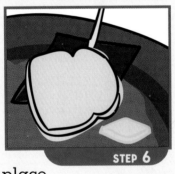
STEP 6

7 Transfer the French toast from the skillet to a baking sheet. Cover lightly with aluminum foil and place in the oven to keep warm while you cook the other slices.

8 Repeat with the remaining slices, being sure to add 1 teaspoon of the butter to the pan before every slice.

9 Sprinkle the French toast with confectioners' sugar and serve with maple syrup or cane sugar if desired.

The freshness of the bread is important. Fresh bread will absorb batter more quickly than stale bread. Depending on the size of the bread, you may find that there's a bit of batter left over. If that's the case, just go ahead, add a bit more butter to the pan, and cook up another slice or two. If you don't want to eat these today, refrigerate them, tightly covered, for up to one or two days, and reheat in the oven or microwave for a really quick breakfast or great afternoon snack!

KICKED-UP SCRAMBLED EGGS

Scrambled eggs are not only simple to make but also a delicious and nutritious way to start the day! I kick them up a bit here by adding some of my Baby Bam and then sprinkling a little grated cheese over the top right before serving—hey, have you ever seen a little cheese hurt anything? One secret to making great scrambled eggs is to stir the eggs continually while they're cooking—this ensures even cooking and a nice, light texture.

Yield
2 SERVINGS

Ingredients
3 LARGE EGGS

2 TABLESPOONS WHOLE MILK

½ TEASPOON BABY BAM (PAGE 234)

⅛ TEASPOON SALT

1 TEASPOON UNSALTED BUTTER

¼ CUP GRATED MILD CHEDDAR CHEESE

Tools
MEASURING SPOONS, SMALL MIXING BOWL, SMALL WHISK OR FORK, GRATER, 6-INCH NONSTICK SKILLET, WOODEN SPOON

Directions

1. Break the eggs one at a time into a small mixing bowl and beat with a whisk or fork.

2. Add the milk, Baby Bam, and salt, and whisk well to combine.

3. Melt the butter in a small skillet over medium-high heat.

4. Add the eggs and cook, stirring constantly with a wooden spoon, until the eggs are just set, about 30 seconds.

5. Sprinkle with the cheese, remove the skillet from the heat, and let rest for 20 to 30 seconds until the cheese melts. Spoon onto two plates and serve immediately.

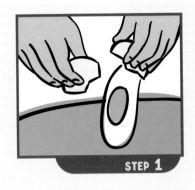

STEP 1

Add chopped ham or crumbled crispy bacon to kick up these already Kicked-Up Scrambled Eggs!

MAKE 'EM PANCAKES

My mom used to make pancakes for me as a kid, and I don't know anyone who doesn't enjoy a good stack of pancakes every now and then. I like to make mine with buttermilk, which gives them an especially delicious flavor and makes them light and tender—but hey, if you'd rather, use milk instead. If you follow this recipe exactly, you'll end up with pancakes that are on the thick side. If you prefer thinner pancakes, simply add a bit more buttermilk (or milk) to the batter.

Yield

ABOUT EIGHTEEN 4-INCH PANCAKES, SERVING 4 TO 6

Ingredients

2 CUPS ALL-PURPOSE FLOUR

2 TEASPOONS SUGAR

2 TEASPOONS BAKING POWDER

½ TEASPOON SALT

2 LARGE EGGS

2½ CUPS BUTTERMILK OR 2¼ CUPS WHOLE MILK

4 TABLESPOONS MELTED UNSALTED BUTTER

2 TABLESPOONS COLD UNSALTED BUTTER

Tools

MEASURING CUPS AND SPOONS, SIFTER, LARGE MIXING BOWL, MEDIUM MIXING BOWL, WIRE WHISK, 10- OR 12-INCH NONSTICK SKILLET, SMALL LADLE (OPTIONAL), PLASTIC TURNER, BAKING SHEET, ALUMINUM FOIL, OVEN MITTS OR POT HOLDERS

CAUTION

Directions

1. Sift the flour, sugar, baking powder, and salt into a large mixing bowl.

2. In a medium mixing bowl, whisk the eggs and the buttermilk until smooth.

STEP 1

3　Add the buttermilk mixture to the sifted dry ingredients along with the melted butter and whisk lightly, just to combine. Be careful not to overmix—and don't worry if there are still some lumps in the batter.

4　Let the batter rest for at least 15 minutes, or tightly cover and refrigerate for up to 8 hours.

5　Preheat the oven to 200°F.

6　Heat a large skillet over medium-high heat until hot.

7　Melt 1 teaspoon of the cold butter in the skillet.

8　With a measuring cup or small ladle, spoon about ¼ cup of the batter into the skillet for each pancake, fitting up to 3 pancakes in the pan without overcrowding. Cook until bubbles form on the surface, about 3 to 4 minutes. (The time will depend on your stove as well as what size skillet you use!) With a plastic turner, carefully turn the pancakes one at a time, and cook until golden brown on the second side, about 2 to 3 minutes.

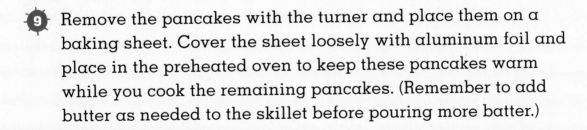
STEP 8

9　Remove the pancakes with the turner and place them on a baking sheet. Cover the sheet loosely with aluminum foil and place in the preheated oven to keep these pancakes warm while you cook the remaining pancakes. (Remember to add butter as needed to the skillet before pouring more batter.)

If you want to kick things up a bit, you can add chopped fruit or nuts (or both!) to the pancake batter. Some of my favorite additions are mashed bananas and chopped walnuts, chopped strawberries, or whole blueberries or raspberries. You can even eat your pancakes with fruit jam layered between them instead of syrup! Some folks I know like to roll their pancakes up around breakfast sausages, too.

GO NUTS FOR BANANA BREAD

Yield
1 LOAF, SERVING 8

Ingredients
1 ½ TEASPOONS VEGETABLE SHORTENING OR UNSALTED BUTTER

3 RIPE BANANAS

2 EGGS

1 CUP PACKED LIGHT BROWN SUGAR

¾ CUP VEGETABLE OIL

½ CUP SOUR CREAM

¾ TEASPOON GROUND CINNAMON

1 TEASPOON BAKING SODA

1 TEASPOON BAKING POWDER

1 TEASPOON VANILLA EXTRACT

½ TEASPOON SALT

¾ CUP CHOPPED WALNUT PIECES

1 ¾ CUPS ALL-PURPOSE FLOUR

Tools
MEASURING CUPS AND SPOONS, CUTTING BOARD, KNIFE, SMALL MIXING BOWL, FORK, LARGE MIXING BOWL, WIRE WHISK, 6 X 9-INCH LOAF PAN, TOOTHPICK, OVEN MITTS OR POT HOLDERS, WIRE RACK

This is a great way to use those really ripe bananas that no one wants to eat! The riper the bananas, the sweeter and better the banana bread will be. This bread makes great toast when spread with a little butter. Or, for a kicked-up sandwich, spread a thin slice of banana bread with some softened cream cheese and top with another thin slice of bread—yum! And if you're into raisins instead of nuts, go ahead and substitute one cup of raisins for the walnuts called for here.

Directions

CAUTION

1. Make sure the oven rack is in the center position and preheat the oven to 350°F.

2. Lightly grease a 6 by 9-inch loaf pan with the vegetable shortening or butter.

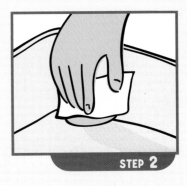
STEP 2

3. Peel the bananas and place in a small mixing bowl. Mash with the back of a fork until there are no big lumps remaining.

4. In a large mixing bowl, combine the eggs, sugar, oil, and sour cream, and whisk until smooth.

STEP 3

5. Add the cinnamon, baking soda, baking powder, vanilla extract, salt, mashed bananas, and walnuts to the egg mixture and whisk to combine.

6. Add the flour and stir until just combined. Do not overmix!

7. Pour the batter into the loaf pan and bake until golden brown and risen, about 1 hour and 10 minutes.

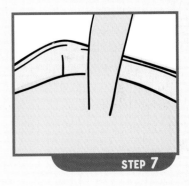
STEP 7

8. Using oven mitts or pot holders, remove the loaf from the oven and let rest for 10 minutes in the pan. Turn out onto a wire rack to finish cooling before serving.

Don't be alarmed when your banana bread splits open on top while it's baking; this is supposed to happen. To be sure your bread is done, perform the toothpick trick (page 27).

Maple-Buttery Corn Muffins

Yield
12 MUFFINS

Ingredients
1¼ CUPS ALL-PURPOSE FLOUR

½ CUP YELLOW CORNMEAL

2 TEASPOONS BAKING POWDER

½ TEASPOON BAKING SODA

½ TEASPOON SALT

2 LARGE EGGS

½ CUP WHOLE MILK

½ CUP SOUR CREAM

¼ CUP MAPLE SYRUP

¼ CUP LIGHT BROWN SUGAR

3 TABLESPOONS MELTED UNSALTED BUTTER

Tools
MEASURING CUPS AND SPOONS, 12-CUP MUFFIN TIN, 12 PAPER MUFFIN-TIN LINERS, MEDIUM MIXING BOWL, LARGE MIXING BOWL, WIRE WHISK, OVEN MITTS OR POT HOLDERS, SMALL SAUCEPAN, WIRE RACK

I grew up in Massachusetts, where maple syrup is used in cooking all kinds of things, from breakfast cereals to baked beans to desserts—you name it. It gives an interesting flavor, and I especially like to add it to baked goods. While you might not think that corn muffins would make a good breakfast treat, just wait till you try these! And once you top them with the maple butter . . . man, oh, man, now you're talking!

Directions

1. Make sure the oven rack is in the center position and preheat the oven to 350°F.

2. Line a 12-cup muffin tin with 12 paper muffin-tin liners.

3. Place the flour, cornmeal, baking powder, baking soda, and salt in a medium mixing bowl and stir to combine.

4. In a large mixing bowl, combine the eggs, milk, sour cream, maple syrup, sugar, and melted butter, and whisk until smooth.

5. Add the dry ingredients to the egg mixture and whisk just until incorporated, being careful not to overmix.

6. Divide the batter evenly among the muffin cups.

7. Bake in the oven until golden brown, about 18 to 20 minutes.

8. Using oven mitts or pot holders, remove the muffins from the oven and let cool in the tin for 5 minutes before turning out onto a wire rack. Serve warm with maple butter.

STEP 2

STEP 6

MAPLE BUTTER

Yield
½ CUP

Ingredients
7 TABLESPOONS UNSALTED BUTTER, SOFTENED

2 TABLESPOONS MAPLE SYRUP

Tools
MEASURING SPOONS, SMALL MIXING BOWL, KNIFE, SMALL WHISK OR FORK, PLASTIC WRAP

Directions

1. In a small mixing bowl, combine the butter and syrup, using a small whisk or fork.

2. Serve with the corn muffins or wrap tightly with plastic wrap and keep refrigerated for up to 2 weeks.

MILE-HIGH BLUEBERRY MUFFINS

Yield

12 MUFFINS

Ingredients

2 CUPS ALL-PURPOSE FLOUR

½ CUP SUGAR

1 ½ TEASPOONS BAKING POWDER

½ TEASPOON BAKING SODA

½ TEASPOON SALT

⅔ CUP PLAIN YOGURT

2 LARGE EGGS

2 TABLESPOONS MELTED UNSALTED BUTTER

2 TEASPOONS GRATED LEMON ZEST (PAGE 21)

1 CUP FRESH OR THAWED FROZEN BLUEBERRIES

½ CUP WHOLE MILK

Tools

MEASURING CUPS AND SPOONS, LEMON ZESTER OR FINE GRATER, 12-CUP MUFFIN TIN, 12 PAPER MUFFIN-TIN LINERS, SIFTER, MEDIUM MIXING BOWL, LARGE MIXING BOWL, WIRE WHISK, RUBBER SPATULA, OVEN MITTS OR POT HOLDERS, SMALL SAUCEPAN, WIRE RACK

These extra-light and fluffy muffins are really awesome in the summer, when blueberries are fresh, and particularly if you pick them yourself right from the bush. If you can't get fresh blueberries, go ahead and use frozen. The only difference you'll find is that the frozen ones break up more when you fold them in and sometimes turn the batter a light purple color.

Directions

CAUTION

1. Make sure the oven rack is in the center position and preheat the oven to 350°F.

2. Line a 12-muffin tin with 12 paper muffin-tin liners.

STEP 2

3. Sift the flour, sugar, baking powder, baking soda, and salt into a medium mixing bowl.

> Sifting is cool—you can put all the dry ingredients into the sifter at once and then just shake or crank!

4. In a large mixing bowl, whisk together the yogurt, eggs, butter, and lemon zest.

5. Add the dry ingredients to the yogurt mixture and whisk just until combined, being careful not to overmix.

STEP 6

6. Using a rubber spatula, gently fold the blueberries into the batter, again being careful not to overmix.

7. Divide the batter evenly among the muffin cups.

8. Bake in the oven until puffed up and golden brown, about 20 to 22 minutes.

STEP 7

9. Using oven mitts or pot holders, remove the muffins from the oven and let cool in the tin for 5 minutes before turning out onto a wire rack. Serve warm.

WAKE-YOU-UP APPLE-CINNAMON MUFFINS

Yield

12 MUFFINS

Ingredients

STREUSEL TOPPING

½ CUP TOASTED CHOPPED WALNUT PIECES (PAGE 233)

½ CUP PACKED LIGHT BROWN SUGAR

¼ CUP ALL-PURPOSE FLOUR

½ TEASPOON GROUND CINNAMON

2 TABLESPOONS MELTED UNSALTED BUTTER

MUFFINS

2 CUPS ALL-PURPOSE FLOUR

1 TEASPOON BAKING POWDER

½ TEASPOON BAKING SODA

½ TEASPOON GROUND CINNAMON

¼ TEASPOON SALT

⅛ TEASPOON GRATED NUTMEG

½ CUP COARSELY CHOPPED DRIED APPLES

½ CUP GRANULATED SUGAR

2 LARGE EGGS

½ CUP WHOLE MILK

1 CUP HOMEMADE APPLESAUCE (PAGE 212) OR STORE-BOUGHT APPLESAUCE

4 TABLESPOONS MELTED UNSALTED BUTTER

Tools

MEASURING CUPS AND SPOONS, CUTTING BOARD, KNIFE, SMALL MIXING BOWL, FORK, 12-CUP MUFFIN TIN, 12 PAPER MUFFIN-TIN LINERS, MEDIUM MIXING BOWL, LARGE MIXING BOWL, WIRE WHISK, OVEN MITTS OR POT HOLDERS, WIRE RACK

I like my apple-cinnamon muffins not too sweet, to let the flavor of the apples really come through, so I make mine with Homemade Applesauce, which is a little less sweet than the store-bought kind. Keep this in mind when you make your muffins. If you're using Homemade Applesauce but you like a sweeter muffin, then you might want to add one or two more tablespoons of sugar to your batter. Hey, it's that simple! And if you're not up to making your own applesauce, store-bought works just fine!

Directions

1 Make sure the oven rack is in the center position and preheat the oven to 350°F.

2 Make the streusel topping by combining the walnuts, brown sugar, ¼ cup flour, and ½ teaspoon cinnamon in a small mixing bowl. Stir with a fork to combine.

3 Add the 2 tablespoons butter and stir well. Set aside while you prepare the muffin batter.

If you're a big raisin fan, kick up your apple-cinnamon muffins by adding some raisins to the muffin batter—you can't go wrong!

4 Line a 12-muffin tin with 12 paper muffin-tin liners.

STEP **4**

5 Place the remaining 2 cups of flour, baking powder, baking soda, the remaining ½ teaspoon of cinnamon, salt, and nutmeg in the medium mixing bowl and stir to combine.

6 Add the apples and granulated sugar and stir well.

7 In a large mixing bowl, whisk together the eggs, milk, applesauce, and melted butter.

8 Add the dry ingredients to the egg mixture and whisk just until incorporated, being careful not to overmix.

9 Divide the batter evenly among the muffin cups.

STEP **9**

10 Sprinkle the streusel topping over the batter, dividing it evenly among the 12 cups.

11 Bake the muffins in the oven until golden brown, about 25 minutes.

12 Using oven mitts or pot holders, remove the muffins from the oven and let cool in the tin for 10 minutes. Serve warm.

STEP **10**

CINNAMON TOAST OF LOVE

Not only a terrific breakfast treat, this cinnamon toast is one of my all-time favorite snacks to eat any time of the day! I like to make my cinnamon toast with white bread because you can really taste the cinnamon sugar that way. But if you like another kind of bread, go ahead and use your favorite. All that sugar and cinnamon and butter on top is going to make just about anything taste great!

Yield

2 TO 4 SERVINGS

Ingredients

4 SLICES WHITE BREAD

2 TABLESPOONS UNSALTED BUTTER, SOFTENED

3½ TABLESPOONS SUGAR

1½ TEASPOONS GROUND CINNAMON

Tools

MEASURING SPOONS, CUTTING BOARD OR LARGE PLATE, BUTTER KNIFE OR OTHER SPREADER, SMALL BOWL, TOASTER OVEN, SPOON, OVEN MITTS OR POT HOLDERS

Directions

CAUTION

1. Place the bread on a cutting board or large plate.

2. With a butter knife or other spreader, spread each slice with about 1½ teaspoons of the butter.

STEP 2

3. Pour the sugar and cinnamon into a small bowl and stir with a spoon to combine well.

4. Sprinkle about 1 tablespoon of the cinnamon sugar over each slice of bread to evenly coat.

5. Place the prepared bread slices directly on the rack of a toaster oven and toast until golden brown and bubbly, about 2 to 3 minutes. Serve warm.

Did you know that cinnamon comes from the inner bark of a tree?

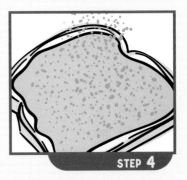
STEP 4

GOOEY CINNAMON BUNS

Yield
20 BUNS

Ingredients
CINNAMON BUNS

1 CUP WHOLE MILK

6 TABLESPOONS GRANULATED SUGAR

1 PACKAGE ACTIVE DRY YEAST

3 CUPS PLUS 2 TABLESPOONS
ALL-PURPOSE FLOUR, PLUS MORE FOR
ROLLING OUT DOUGH

½ TEASPOON SALT

6 TABLESPOONS UNSALTED BUTTER,
SOFTENED

1 EGG

½ CUP RAISINS

1 TEASPOON VEGETABLE OIL

NUTTY FILLING

¾ CUP PACKED LIGHT BROWN SUGAR

½ CUP CHOPPED WALNUTS OR
PECANS

2 TABLESPOONS PLUS
2 TEASPOONS GROUND
CINNAMON

½ TEASPOON SALT

12 TABLESPOONS MELTED
UNSALTED BUTTER

Tools

MEASURING CUPS AND SPOONS,
CUTTING BOARD, SMALL SAUCEPAN,
INSTANT-READ THERMOMETER,
2 SMALL MIXING BOWLS, WIRE
WHISK, SIFTER, 2 LARGE MIXING
BOWLS, LARGE WOODEN SPOON,
STANDING ELECTRIC MIXER WITH
DOUGH HOOK (OPTIONAL),
PLASTIC WRAP, ROLLING PIN,
RULER, SMALL SPOON, SHARP
KNIFE, LARGE NONSTICK BAKING
SHEET, MEDIUM MIXING BOWL,
OVEN MITTS OR POT HOLDERS

Man, oh, man, I just have to tell you how awesome these cinnamon buns are, especially when they're still warm and gooey, with their sweet glaze dripping everywhere. You will see that there are several steps to making these buns, but they are without a doubt well worth the effort. If you want to make some friends real fast, this is definitely the ticket.

Directions

CAUTION

1 Place the milk in a small saucepan. Heat over medium-low heat until the milk is warm, about 110°F on an instant-read thermometer. Remove from the heat.

2 Combine 2 tablespoons of the granulated sugar with the yeast in a small mixing bowl, whisk in the warm milk, and let rest until slightly thickened and foamy, about 5 minutes. This lets you know that the yeast is working.

3 Sift the flour, the remaining 4 tablespoons of granulated sugar, and the salt into a large mixing bowl. Add the softened butter, egg, raisins, and the yeast mixture, stirring well with a large wooden spoon to incorporate all of the flour.

4 Place the dough on a work surface sprinkled with 2 tablespoons of flour and knead until smooth and elastic, about 3 to 5 minutes (see page 26). The dough should not be sticky—if it is, add a bit more flour and continue kneading to work it into the dough. (Alternately, mix the dough in an electric mixer fitted with a dough hook.)

5 Using your hands, form the dough into a ball and lightly grease it with the vegetable oil.

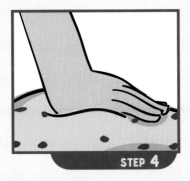
STEP **4**

STEP **5**

6 Place the dough into a large mixing bowl and cover with plastic wrap. Let rest in a warm, draft-free place and allow to rise until doubled in size, about 1½ hours.

7 When the dough has risen, divide it into two equal portions.

8 In a small mixing bowl, make the nutty filling by combining the brown sugar, nuts, cinnamon, salt, and melted butter, and stirring until smooth.

9 Place one portion of the dough on a lightly floured surface and sprinkle with a little bit more flour, then use a rolling pin to roll it into a large rectangle, about 12 inches by 9 inches.

STEP 9

10 Using the back of a small spoon, carefully spread half of the nutty filling over the top of the dough.

When rolling out dough and cutting it into portions, measuring with a ruler helps ensure good results!

11 With the long end of the rectangle facing you, roll up the dough into a tight cylinder.

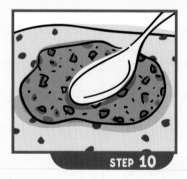

STEP 10

STEP 11

12 Pinch the edges together and use a sharp knife to cut 1-inch-thick slices.

STEP 12

13. Place the rounds on a large baking sheet, leaving half an inch between the rounds.

STEP 13

14. Repeat with the remaining dough.

15. Cover rounds with plastic wrap and let rest in a warm, draft-free place until risen by half their size and almost touching, 30 to 60 minutes.

16. Make sure the oven rack is in the center position and preheat the oven to 350°F.

17. Bake until golden brown, about 25 to 30 minutes.

18. Combine the glaze ingredients in a medium mixing bowl and stir until smooth.

19. Using oven mitts or pot holders, remove buns from the oven and drizzle the glaze over the tops. Serve warm.

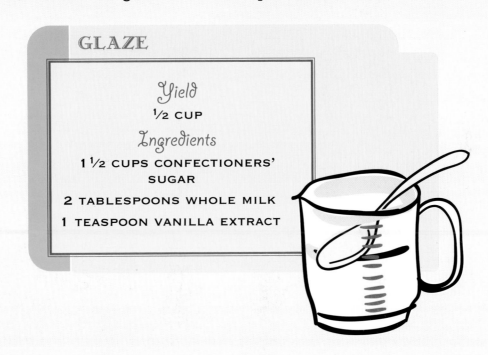

GLAZE

Yield
½ CUP

Ingredients
1 ½ CUPS CONFECTIONERS' SUGAR
2 TABLESPOONS WHOLE MILK
1 TEASPOON VANILLA EXTRACT

Yummy Wake-Up Smoothies

This is one surefire way to get you started in the morning! And good for you, too! (Hey, if you like this as much as I bet you will, you'll also want it for snacks.) Don't worry; go right ahead, because all this fresh fruit and yogurt will pick you up just about any time of the day!

Yield
ABOUT 3 CUPS, SERVING 2 TO 4

Ingredients
1 LARGE RIPE BANANA, PEELED AND SLICED

1 CUP WASHED STRAWBERRIES, STEMS AND HULLS REMOVED (PAGE 20)

½ CUP RASPBERRIES OR PEELED AND SLICED KIWIS (ABOUT 2 KIWIS)

1 CUP PLAIN YOGURT

¼ CUP ORANGE JUICE

2 TABLESPOONS HONEY

Tools
MEASURING CUPS AND SPOONS, CUTTING BOARD, PARING KNIFE, BLENDER

Directions

Make sure the blender lid is on snugly!

1 Place all of the ingredients in the blender and process on high speed until smooth, about 30 to 45 seconds.

STEP 1

2 Pour into glasses and serve.

Feel free to substitute or add other fruits, such as blueberries, mangoes, or peaches. And feel free to substitute pineapple juice for the orange juice—it'll work just as well!

IT-ISN'T-ROCKET-SCIENCE SALADS

CHAPTER 2

SIMPLY SENSATIONAL TUNA SALAD

Yield
2 CUPS, SERVING 4 TO 6

Ingredients
2 (6-OUNCE) CANS WATER-PACKED CHUNK WHITE TUNA

2 TABLESPOONS MAYONNAISE

2 TABLESPOONS QUICK-AND-CREAMY HERB DRESSING (PAGE 67), OR STORE-BOUGHT RANCH DRESSING

2 TABLESPOONS FINELY CHOPPED CELERY

2 TABLESPOONS FINELY CHOPPED YELLOW ONION

1 TEASPOON BABY BAM (PAGE 234)

Tools
MEASURING SPOONS, CAN OPENER, FINE MESH STRAINER, SPOON, LARGE MIXING BOWL, FORK

There are lots of ways you can serve this: on top of lettuce leaves, on sliced tomatoes, even inside a halved, seeded avocado. Or scoop the pulp out of a tomato, and serve the tuna salad inside! Another idea is to make little baby sandwiches out of crackers or toasted bread. If you're in the mood for something really gooey and yummy, kick things up another notch by turning to page 116 for my Tuna Melts in Your Mouth! Oh yeah, baby!

56

Directions

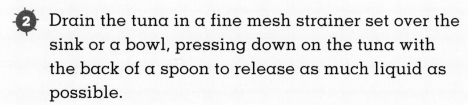

CAUTION

Be extra careful when opening cans—the lids can cut like a knife!

1. Open the cans of tuna, being very careful with the sharp lids.

2. Drain the tuna in a fine mesh strainer set over the sink or a bowl, pressing down on the tuna with the back of a spoon to release as much liquid as possible.

3. Place the drained tuna in a large mixing bowl.

4. Add the remaining ingredients and mix well with a fork.

5. Serve in a sandwich or inside a scooped-out tomato.

STEP **2**

Kick up your tuna salad by adding chopped hard-boiled eggs! (See page 99 for how to boil eggs.)

OPTIONAL ACCOMPANIMENTS

Lettuce leaves	Scooped-out tomato
Sliced tomatoes	Cucumber slices
Halved or sliced avocados	Toasted crackers

DRESS-UP PASTA SALAD

Yield

ABOUT 10 CUPS,
SERVING 10 TO 12

Ingredients

1 POUND BOW-TIE
PASTA

¾ CUP GRATED
PARMESAN CHEESE

2 TABLESPOONS
BASIL PESTO (PAGE
132), OR TO TASTE

¼ CUP EXTRA-
VIRGIN OLIVE OIL,
OR TO TASTE

¾ TEASPOON BABY
BAM (PAGE 234)

½ TEASPOON SALT

Tools

MEASURING CUPS
AND SPOONS,
GRATER, 5- OR
6-QUART HEAVY POT
WITH LID, OVEN
MITTS OR POT
HOLDERS, LARGE
COLANDER, LARGE
MIXING BOWL,
LARGE WOODEN
SPOON, PLASTIC
WRAP (OPTIONAL)

This is one of those basic recipes that should
serve as a jumping-off point for you. I call it Dress-Up
Pasta Salad because I make it with that fancy bow-tie
pasta and because it's just begging to be "dressed up"
by additions such as halved cherry tomatoes, peas,
roasted bell peppers, chopped green onions, blanched
asparagus, goat cheese,
Parmesan cheese,
chopped black
olives, marinated
artichoke hearts,
chopped sun-
dried tomatoes,
toasted pine
nuts—you name
it! Let your taste
buds be your guide!

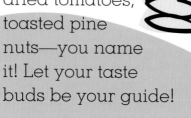

Directions

CAUTION

1 Bring a large, heavy pot of salted water to a boil over high heat.

2 Add the pasta and return to a low boil. Reduce heat to medium-low and cook pasta according to the package directions, about 10 minutes, stirring occasionally to prevent the pasta from sticking together. Don't overcook!

3 Using oven mitts or pot holders, drain the pasta in a colander set in the sink, pouring away from you. Rinse with cold water until the pasta is cool and allow to drain in the sink for 10 minutes.

STEP 3

4 Place the pasta in a large mixing bowl.

5 Toss with the remaining ingredients, stirring well with a large wooden spoon.

6 If desired, add optional ingredients (below).

7 Serve at room temperature or cover tightly with plastic wrap and refrigerate until ready to serve.

You can really kick this up by adding any (or all) of the following:

OPTIONAL ACCOMPANIMENTS

Cherry tomatoes	Artichoke hearts
Chopped tomatoes	Cooked and drained white
Blanched asparagus	beans or green peas
Other cheeses, such as goat	Red or green bell peppers,
cheese and feta cheese	chopped, sliced, or roasted
Chopped black olives	Thinly sliced red onion
Chopped sun-dried tomatoes	

YOUR FAVORITE FRUIT SALAD

Yield

8 CUPS, SERVING
8 TO 10

Ingredients

8 CUPS OF YOUR
FAVORITE FRUITS,
CHOPPED, SUCH AS:

1 CUP HONEYDEW
MELON IN 1-INCH
CUBES

1 CUP CANTALOUPE
IN 1-INCH CUBES

1 CUP ORANGE
SEGMENTS

1 CUP RED GRAPES

1 CUP BANANA
SLICES

1 CUP CORED AND
CHOPPED APPLE

1 CUP BLUEBERRIES

1 CUP HULLED AND
SLICED
STRAWBERRIES

½ CUP PLAIN
YOGURT

1 TABLESPOON FRESH
LEMON JUICE

1 TABLESPOON FRESH
ORANGE JUICE

½ CUP TOASTED
COCONUT (PAGE 233)

Tools

MEASURING CUPS
AND SPOONS,
CUTTING BOARD,
KNIFE, CORER, LARGE
MIXING BOWL, LARGE
SPOON

It's important to choose fruits that you really like, as well as fruits that are in season, for this simple salad. If you're lucky enough to get fruits at their peak of ripeness, odds are you won't need to add anything extra to this salad to make it super yummy. However, if you're in the mood for something a little sweeter, try adding a tablespoon or two of honey— it should do just the trick.

Directions

CAUTION

1 Combine all the fruit in a large mixing bowl.

STEP **1**

2 Add the yogurt, lemon juice, and orange juice to the fruit and stir with a large spoon to combine.

3 Divide the fruit salad among serving plates or bowls, sprinkle each serving with some of the toasted coconut, and serve.

Try serving your fruit salad with a scoop of ice cream or frozen yogurt—or even a dollop of vanilla- or fruit-flavored yogurt, topped with a little Crispy-Crunchy Granola Munchies (page 120) for crunch!

Nutty Apple Salad

Here's a great dish to make for your next family picnic or barbecue. This salad is deliciously crunchy, and the fresh apple and celery flavors go well with lots of different things. This recipe makes a whole lot, so if you don't have a big enough group to eat this much, just cut the recipe in half. Hey, it's not rocket science, you know. Oh, and one last thing: If you're a cheese fan, like I am, you might want to add some crumbled blue cheese (like Maytag Blue) or goat cheese to your salad to really take it over the top!

Yield
ABOUT 7 CUPS, SERVING 8 TO 10

Ingredients
2 ROME OR FUJI APPLES

2 GOLDEN DELICIOUS APPLES

1 ½ CUPS TOASTED WALNUT PIECES (PAGE 233)

2 STALKS CELERY, TRIMMED AND SLICED (ABOUT 1 CUP)

⅓ CUP RAISINS

3 TABLESPOONS MAYONNAISE

2 TABLESPOONS FRESH LEMON JUICE

2 TABLESPOONS RICE WINE VINEGAR

½ TEASPOON SALT

Tools
MEASURING CUPS AND SPOONS, CUTTING BOARD, APPLE CORER, KNIFE, LARGE MIXING BOWL, LARGE SPOON

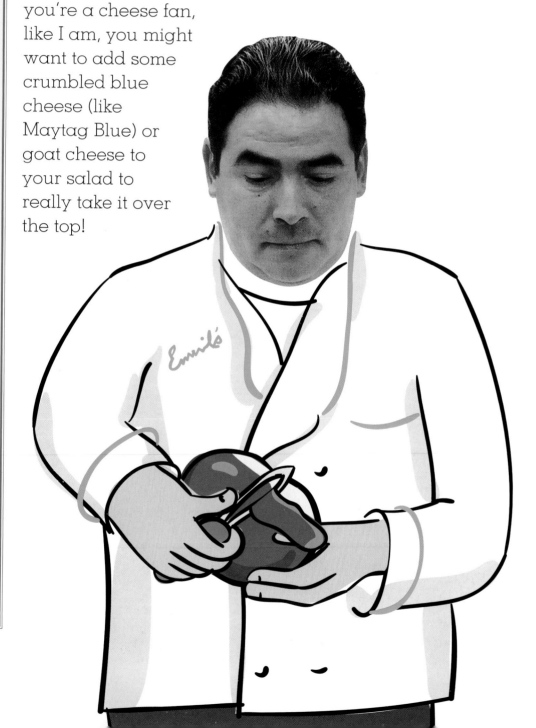

Directions

STEP 1

1. Place the apples on a cutting board and core (page 20). Cut one apple in half. Place one apple half, flat side down, on the cutting board and cut lengthwise into quarters. Cut the quarters into ½-inch pieces and place in a large mixing bowl.

2. Repeat with the other apple half and the remaining apples.

3. Add the walnuts, celery, raisins, mayonnaise, lemon juice, vinegar, and salt, and stir well.

4. Serve immediately or cover tightly with plastic wrap and refrigerate for up to 6 hours.

Lemon juice is often added to cut-up fruit—lemons contain a special acid, called citric acid, which prevents fruit from turning brown. The juice of other citrus fruits (like oranges and limes), as well as pineapple juice and the juice of some berries, will have the same effect.

You-Pick-the-Greens Salad with Three Simple Dressings

Yield
6 to 8 servings

Ingredients
8 cups assorted salad greens, such as romaine, iceberg, bibb, red leaf, green leaf, watercress, mesclun, arugula, endive

Optional Accompaniments
Carrot sticks or grated carrots, sliced celery, tomatoes, thinly sliced onion rings, peeled and sliced cucumber, chopped or sliced red or green bell pepper, croutons, grated or crumbled cheese

¾ cup dressing of choice

Tools
Measuring cups, cutting board, knife, clean dish towel, salad spinner or colander, large mixing bowl or decorative salad bowl, damp towel or plastic wrap, salad servers or large fork and spoon

Here's a recipe where you get to make all the decisions: what type of lettuce, what type of dressing, whether or not to add vegetables or croutons, and whether to serve the salad in a pretty bowl at the table or to toss and plate up everything in the kitchen. Just make it up as you go along, remembering to add a little more dressing for each topping.

1. Remove and discard any wilted, brown, or discolored outer leaves from the greens.

2. Place the greens on a cutting board and cut off the stems or cores with a knife.

STEP 1

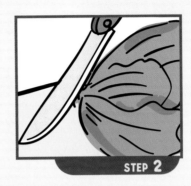

STEP 2

3. Fill a clean kitchen sink with cold water.

4. Separate the leaves and place in the sinkful of water.

5. Swirl the greens with your hands to remove any dirt or debris.

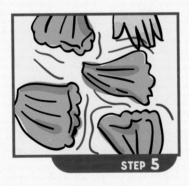

STEP 5

6. Place the washed greens on a clean dish towel.

7. In batches, dry the greens in a salad spinner. (If you don't have a salad spinner, simply place the leaves in a colander and allow them to drain.)

8. Tear the greens with your hands into bite-size pieces and place in a large mixing bowl or decorative salad bowl. Cover with a damp towel or plastic wrap and refrigerate until ready to serve.

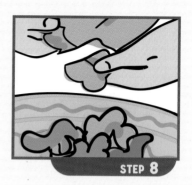

STEP 8

9. Add optional ingredients as desired, toss with dressing, and serve immediately.

TANGY VINAIGRETTE DRESSING

Yield
ABOUT 1¼ CUPS

Ingredients
1 TEASPOON BABY BAM (PAGE 234)

1 TEASPOON EMERIL'S ITALIAN ESSENCE OR OTHER ITALIAN HERB BLEND

1½ TEASPOONS DIJON MUSTARD

1 TABLESPOON SUGAR

¼ CUP CHAMPAGNE (OR WHITE WINE) VINEGAR

2 TABLESPOONS FINELY CHOPPED GREEN ONIONS (TOPS ONLY)

¾ CUP VEGETABLE OIL

Tools
MEASURING CUPS AND SPOONS, LARGE MIXING BOWL, WIRE WHISK, NONREACTIVE CONTAINER

Directions

1. In a large mixing bowl, combine Baby Bam, Emeril's Italian Essence, mustard, sugar, vinegar, and green onions, and whisk to combine.

2. While continuing to whisk, slowly drizzle the oil into the vinegar mixture, little by little, until thoroughly combined.

3. Serve immediately over salad or transfer to a nonreactive container, cover tightly, and refrigerate until ready to use, up to 1 week.

QUICK-AND-CREAMY HERB DRESSING

Yield
1 ½ CUPS

Ingredients
½ CUP BUTTERMILK

½ CUP SOUR CREAM

¼ CUP MAYONNAISE

¼ CUP MINCED GREEN ONIONS (TOPS ONLY)

1 TABLESPOON MINCED FRESH PARSLEY

⅛ TEASPOON GROUND BLACK PEPPER

¾ TEASPOON SALT

1 TEASPOON MINCED GARLIC

2 TEASPOONS FRESH LEMON JUICE

½ TEASPOON BABY BAM (PAGE 234)

Tools
MEASURING CUPS AND SPOONS, CUTTING BOARD, KNIFE, GARLIC PRESS (OPTIONAL), LARGE MIXING BOWL, WIRE WHISK, AIRTIGHT CONTAINER

Directions

1 Place all the ingredients in a large mixing bowl.

2 Whisk until smooth.

3 Serve immediately over salad or pour into a container, cover tightly, and refrigerate until needed, up to 1 week.

EASY FRENCH DRESSING

Yield
1 ¼ CUPS

Ingredients
½ CUP MAYONNAISE

½ CUP KETCHUP

1 TABLESPOON MINCED YELLOW ONION

2 TEASPOONS WHITE VINEGAR

2 TEASPOONS SWEET PAPRIKA

1 TEASPOON WORCESTERSHIRE SAUCE

½ TEASPOON MINCED GARLIC

½ TEASPOON BABY BAM (PAGE 234)

Tools
MEASURING CUPS AND SPOONS, CUTTING BOARD, KNIFE, GARLIC PRESS (OPTIONAL), LARGE MIXING BOWL, WIRE WHISK, AIRTIGHT CONTAINER

Directions

1 Place all the ingredients in a large mixing bowl.

2 Whisk until smooth.

3 Serve immediately over salad or pour into a container, cover tightly, and refrigerate until needed, up to 1 week.

These dressings are great on top of a green salad, as we've suggested, but they also work well as dips for veggies and spreads for extra-special sandwiches. Be creative!

"P" IS FOR PIZZA AND PASTA

CHAPTER 3

Best Basic Red Sauce

Yield
**10 CUPS
(2½ QUARTS)**

Ingredients
2 TABLESPOONS OLIVE
OIL

1½ CUPS CHOPPED
YELLOW ONION

1 TEASPOON MINCED
GARLIC

½ TEASPOON SALT

½ TEASPOON DRIED
BASIL

½ TEASPOON DRIED
OREGANO

⅛ TEASPOON GROUND
BLACK PEPPER

2 (28-OUNCE) CANS
WHOLE PEELED
TOMATOES

2 (15-OUNCE) CANS
TOMATO SAUCE

3 TABLESPOONS
TOMATO PASTE

2 CUPS WATER

1 TEASPOON SUGAR

Tools
MEASURING CUPS AND
SPOONS, CUTTING
BOARD, KNIFE, GARLIC
PRESS (OPTIONAL),
CAN OPENER, 5-QUART
HEAVY POT, LARGE
MIXING BOWL, LONG-
HANDLED WOODEN
SPOON, OVEN MITTS
OR POT HOLDERS,
AIRTIGHT CONTAINER

This sauce is really easy and really yummy, and once you've made a big ol' batch of this, you've got lots of options: pizza, spaghetti and meatballs, lasagne—you name it! I like to use canned whole tomatoes instead of chopped tomatoes or tomato puree when making my Best Basic Red Sauce. Not only is it fun to squeeze and break up the tomatoes by hand, but the sauce also has a much better texture if you use whole tomatoes.

Directions

Be careful when stirring—hot sauce makes bubbles that pop and splatter!

1 Heat the olive oil in a large, heavy pot over medium heat.

2 Add the onions, garlic, salt, basil, oregano, and pepper, and cook, stirring, until soft, about 5 minutes.

3 Place the tomatoes in a large mixing bowl and squeeze with spoon or hands to break them into small pieces.

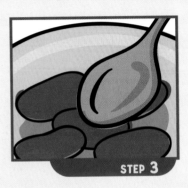

STEP 3

4 Add the tomatoes, tomato sauce, tomato paste, water, and sugar to the pot with the onion and stir well.

5 Bring to a simmer over medium-high heat.

6 Lower the heat to medium-low and simmer, uncovered, for 45 minutes, stirring occasionally with a long-handled wooden spoon.

7 Using oven mitts or pot holders, remove the pot from the heat and use the sauce as needed. You can store this sauce in an airtight container in the refrigerator for up to 4 days, or freeze it for up to 3 months.

Remember that cleaning is an important part of cooking—if you squirt juice when squeezing the tomatoes, make sure to clean it up!

1-2-3 LASAGNE

Yield
8 TO 10 SERVINGS

Ingredients
1 (15-OUNCE)
CONTAINER RICOTTA
CHEESE

2 LARGE EGGS

1 CUP GRATED
PARMESAN CHEESE

4 CUPS GRATED
MOZZARELLA CHEESE
(ABOUT 1 POUND)

1 TEASPOON BABY
BAM (PAGE 234)

½ TEASPOON SALT

2 TEASPOONS DRIED
PARSLEY

1 TEASPOON DRIED
BASIL

¼ TEASPOON GROUND
BLACK PEPPER

5 CUPS BEST BASIC
RED SAUCE (PAGE 70)
OR STORE-BOUGHT
PASTA SAUCE

12 DRIED LASAGNA
NOODLES

Tools
MEASURING CUPS AND
SPOONS, GRATER,
LARGE MIXING BOWL,
LARGE WOODEN
SPOON, 3-QUART (13 x
9 x 2-INCH)
CASSEROLE DISH,
SPATULA, ALUMINUM
FOIL, OVEN MITTS OR
POT HOLDERS

This delicious, cheesy lasagne is super easy to make because you don't cook the noodles first but use them right out of the box! I make mine with Best Basic Red Sauce, but to simplify things, you could make yours with store-bought pasta sauce.

Directions

1 Make sure the oven rack is in the center position and preheat the oven to 375°F.

2 In a large bowl, using a large wooden spoon, stir together the ricotta cheese, eggs, ½ cup of the grated Parmesan cheese, ½ cup of the grated mozzarella cheese, the Baby Bam, salt, parsley, basil, and pepper until thoroughly combined.

3 Spread 1 cup of the Best Basic Red Sauce in the bottom of a 3-quart casserole dish. Lay 3 lasagna noodles lengthwise in the dish. The noodles should not overlap or touch one another. Spoon ¾ cup of the ricotta mixture over the noodles and spread it evenly with a spatula. Sprinkle 1 cup of the mozzarella cheese evenly over the ricotta. Repeat with the remaining ingredients, for a total of 4 layers of noodles. Sprinkle the remaining 1 cup of mozzarella cheese over the top layer of tomato sauce. Top with the remaining ½ cup of Parmesan cheese.

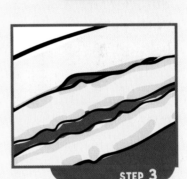

STEP **3**

STEP **3**

4 Cover the casserole tightly with aluminum foil.

5 Bake, covered, for 1 hour.

6 Using oven mitts or pot holders, remove the casserole from the oven and discard the aluminum foil. Return the dish to the oven and bake, uncovered, for 10 minutes.

STEP **3**

7 Using the mitts or pot holders, remove the casserole from the oven and let it rest for 10 minutes before serving.

Watch your fingers when grating cheese!
Have a grown-up help you take the cooked lasagne out of the oven—it's really hot and heavy!

YOU GOTTA LOVE SPAGHETTI AND MEATBALLS

MEATBALLS

Yield

32 MEATBALLS, SERVING 6 TO 8

Ingredients

10 CUPS BEST BASIC RED SAUCE (PAGE 70) OR STORE-BOUGHT PASTA SAUCE

1 LARGE EGG

1 POUND LEAN GROUND BEEF

½ CUP CHOPPED YELLOW ONION

1 TEASPOON MINCED GARLIC

½ TEASPOON DRIED BASIL

½ TEASPOON DRIED OREGANO

½ TEASPOON DRIED PARSLEY

¼ TEASPOON GROUND BLACK PEPPER

2 TEASPOONS YELLOW MUSTARD

1 TEASPOON KETCHUP

½ TEASPOON BABY BAM SEASONING (PAGE 234)

½ TEASPOON SALT

Tools

MEASURING CUPS AND SPOONS, CUTTING BOARD, KNIFE, GARLIC PRESS (OPTIONAL), 5-QUART HEAVY POT, LARGE MIXING BOWL, LONG-HANDLED WOODEN SPOON, OVEN MITTS OR POT HOLDERS

Man, are meatballs ever fun to make! And don't worry if yours aren't a perfect circle; no matter what shape you make them, they're going to taste terrific. I don't cook my meatballs before adding them to the pot; I just plop them in when the sauce is ready. But make sure you don't stir them for at least ten minutes, so they don't break apart. When they start to come to the top of the pot, that's when you'll know they're cooked enough for you to stir.

Directions

C A U T I O N

1. Pour the Best Basic Red Sauce into a large, heavy pot.

2. Bring to a simmer over medium-high heat, stirring occasionally.

3. Place all the remaining meatball ingredients in a large mixing bowl. Stir well with a long-handled wooden spoon to combine.

4. Wash your hands, then roll 1 tablespoon of meat between them to form meatballs. Place meatballs on a plate as they are formed. (Hint: If your hands are slightly damp, the meatballs will roll more easily and will not stick to them!)

STEP 4

5. When all the meatballs are shaped, wash your hands again and then gently place the balls into the sauce one by one, using the long-handled wooden spoon. Be careful—bubbling sauce splatters!

STEP 5

6. Simmer the sauce, uncovered, and allow the meatballs to rest undisturbed for 10 minutes before stirring. When the meatballs rise to the top, it's okay to stir.

7. Stir the sauce and meatballs. Simmer for an additional 20 minutes and stir occasionally to prevent the sauce from sticking to the bottom of the pot.

8. Using oven mitts or pot holders, remove the sauce from the heat and serve immediately over cooked spaghetti.

SPAGHETTI

Yield

4 TO 8 SERVINGS

Ingredients

1 TEASPOON SALT

1 TEASPOON OLIVE OIL

1 POUND SPAGHETTI

Tools

MEASURING SPOONS,
5- TO 6-QUART HEAVY
POT, LONG-HANDLED
WOODEN SPOON, OVEN
MITTS OR POT
HOLDERS, COLANDER

1 Bring a second large, heavy pot of water to a rolling boil over high heat. Add the salt, oil, and spaghetti.

2 Reduce the heat to medium and cook for 10 minutes, stirring occasionally to prevent the spaghetti from sticking together.

3 Using oven mitts or pot holders, remove the pot from the heat and drain the spaghetti in a colander set in the sink, pouring away from you.

4 Add the spaghetti to the pot with the meatballs and sauce and toss to combine. Serve immediately.

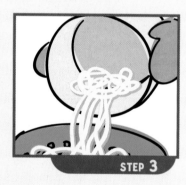

STEP **3**

If you really want all of your meatballs to be the same size, try using a spoon or small scoop to portion out the meat mixture before rolling it into meatballs!

And here's another trick: If you don't plan on serving all of your spaghetti the first night, toss the leftover noodles with a teaspoon or so of olive oil to prevent them from sticking together. This way you can reheat the spaghetti in a pot or the microwave the next day.

MY-OH-MY SPAGHETTI PIE

This layered pie is a really kicked-up idea for leftover spaghetti noodles! I use mozzarella cheese in this recipe, but go ahead and make yours with whatever cheese you like best. Cheddar, Monterey Jack, or even smoked Gouda would be great.

Yield
6 TO 8 SERVINGS

Ingredients

1 ¼ TEASPOONS SALT

2 CUPS BROCCOLI, CUT INTO SMALL FLOWERETS BY USING ONLY ABOUT AN INCH OF THE STEM

2 TEASPOONS OLIVE OIL

1 CUP CHOPPED YELLOW ONION

2 TEASPOON MINCED GARLIC

2 ½ TEASPOONS Baby Bam (PAGE 234)

1 TEASPOON DRIED PARSLEY

½ TEASPOON DRIED BASIL

¼ TEASPOON GROUND BLACK PEPPER

½ POUND GROUND BEEF

8 LARGE EGGS

½ CUP MILK

½ CUP FINELY GRATED Parmesan CHEESE (ABOUT 2 OUNCES)

3 CUPS COOKED SPAGHETTI

1 HEAPING CUP GRATED MOZZARELLA CHEESE (ABOUT 4 OUNCES)

Tools

MEASURING CUPS AND SPOONS, CUTTING BOARD, KNIFE, GRATER, GARLIC PRESS (OPTIONAL), 2 ½-QUART SAUCEPAN, OVEN MITTS OR POT HOLDERS, COLANDER, MEDIUM SKILLET, LARGE MIXING BOWL, WIRE WHISK, 2-QUART CASSEROLE DISH, FORK

Directions

CAUTION

1 Make sure the oven rack is in the center position and preheat the oven to 375°F.

2 Bring a small saucepan of water to a boil over high heat.

3 Add ½ teaspoon of the salt and the broccoli and cook for 3 minutes, until the broccoli is slightly cooked but still crisp and bright green. This is called blanching.

4 Using oven mitts or pot holders, remove the saucepan from the heat and drain the broccoli in a colander set in the sink, pouring away from you. Rinse under cold running water. Set aside to drain.

5 Heat the oil in a medium skillet over medium heat. Add the onions, garlic, 1 teaspoon of the Baby Bam, the parsley, basil, ¼ teaspoon of the remaining salt, the pepper, and ground meat, and cook, stirring, until the meat is no longer pink (that means it's cooked through) and the onions start to brown, about 8 minutes.

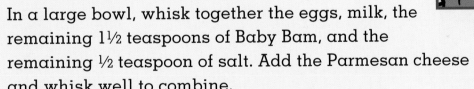

6 In a large bowl, whisk together the eggs, milk, the remaining 1½ teaspoons of Baby Bam, and the remaining ½ teaspoon of salt. Add the Parmesan cheese and whisk well to combine.

7 Spread the cooked spaghetti evenly in a casserole dish.

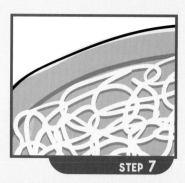

STEP 7

8 Pour the meat mixture over the spaghetti and toss with a fork to combine.

STEP 8

9 Place the blanched broccoli on top of the spaghetti.

STEP 9

10 Pour the egg mixture over the spaghetti.

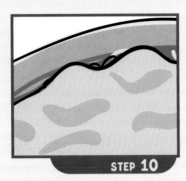

11 Sprinkle the spaghetti evenly with the mozzarella cheese and bake it in the oven until golden brown, about 20 to 25 minutes.

12 Using oven mitts or pot holders, remove the casserole dish from the oven and let it rest and firm for 5 minutes before serving.

Have a grown-up help you take the skillet from the stove and pour the meat into the casserole. Be careful carrying the full casserole dish to the oven and placing it inside—and even more careful taking it out of the oven! It's heavy!

Rock-'n'-Rollin' Rotini Bake

Talk about a great combination: noodles, Best Basic Red Sauce, pork sausage, and lots of cheese. I love rotini—all those curly, twisty parts mean lots of room for sauce and cheese! All you need to add are a salad and a hot loaf of I-Love-Gaaahlic Bread (page 84), and you've got a terrific dinner.

Yield

6 TO 8 SERVINGS

Ingredients

1 TEASPOON SALT

1 TABLESPOON PLUS ½ TEASPOON OLIVE OIL

½ POUND DRIED ROTINI NOODLES

½ POUND PORK BREAKFAST SAUSAGE, REMOVED FROM CASINGS (PAGE 22)

1 CUP CHOPPED YELLOW ONION

2 TEASPOONS MINCED GARLIC

½ TEASPOON BABY BAM (PAGE 234)

¼ TEASPOON GROUND BLACK PEPPER

3 CUPS BEST BASIC RED SAUCE (PAGE 70) OR STORE-BOUGHT PASTA SAUCE

2 CUPS GRATED MOZZARELLA CHEESE (ABOUT ½ POUND)

Tools

MEASURING CUPS AND SPOONS, CUTTING BOARD, KNIFE, GRATER, GARLIC PRESS (OPTIONAL), 5- TO 6-QUART POT, LONG-HANDLED WOODEN SPOON, OVEN MITTS OR POT HOLDERS, COLANDER, MEDIUM SKILLET, 2-QUART CASSEROLE DISH

Directions

Always have an adult help you remove things from the oven—especially a big casserole filled with hot, bubbly food. It's really heavy!

1 Make sure the oven rack is in the center position and preheat the oven to 350°F.

2 Bring a large pot of water to a boil over high heat. Add ½ teaspoon of the salt, ½ teaspoon of the oil, and the rotini. Lower the heat to medium and cook until the pasta is tender yet still firm, about 9 to 10 minutes, stirring occasionally with a long-handled wooden spoon.

3 Using oven mitts or pot holders, remove the pot from the heat and drain the pasta in a colander set in the sink, pouring away from you, and rinse under cold running water. Allow to drain. (You should have 5 cups of cooked pasta.)

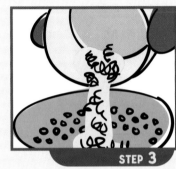

4 Heat the remaining oil in a medium skillet over medium heat. Add the sausage meat and cook, stirring, for 5 minutes. Add the onions, garlic, the remaining ½ teaspoon of salt, the Baby Bam, and pepper, and cook until the meat is brown and the onions are soft, about 5 minutes. Remove from the heat.

5 Evenly spread the cooked noodles in a casserole dish. Add the meat mixture, the Best Basic Red Sauce, and 1 cup of the cheese, and stir to combine thoroughly. Sprinkle the remaining 1 cup of cheese over the pasta. Bake for 25 minutes.

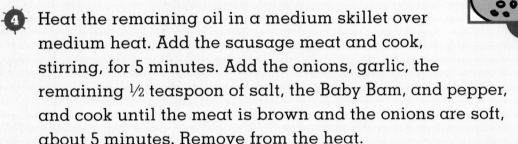

STEP 5

6 Using the mitts or pot holders, carefully remove the casserole from the oven and let it rest for 5 minutes before serving.

Be creative! If you like other pasta shapes better, go for it! Ziti, fusilli, macaroni, or penne rigate all would work just fine for this dish.

I-Love-Gaaahlic Bread

Yield

1 LARGE LOAF,
SERVING 6 TO 8 AS A
SIDE DISH

Ingredients

1 LOAF FRENCH OR
ITALIAN BREAD, ABOUT
22 INCHES LONG

12 TABLESPOONS
(1½ STICKS)
UNSALTED BUTTER,
SOFTENED

2 TABLESPOONS
EXTRA-VIRGIN OLIVE
OIL

½ CUP GRATED
PARMESAN CHEESE

2 TEASPOONS BABY
BAM (PAGE 234)

2 TEASPOONS MINCED
GARLIC

1 TEASPOON DRIED
PARSLEY

¼ TEASPOON SALT

Tools

MEASURING CUPS AND
SPOONS, CUTTING
BOARD, GRATER,
GARLIC PRESS
(OPTIONAL), LARGE
BAKING SHEET,
ALUMINUM FOIL,
SERRATED BREAD
KNIFE, MIXING BOWL,
SPATULA, BUTTER
KNIFE OR OTHER
SPREADER, OVEN
MITTS OR POT
HOLDERS

Talk about amazing—this bread right out of the oven is just unbelievably good! I know a little girl named Alexandra who is only two years old who ate five pieces all by herself! I use minced garlic in this recipe; mincing is really simple to do with a garlic press—or with a knife, if you're supervised. If you find it easier, feel free to substitute about one teaspoon of garlic powder for the fresh garlic, but it won't be as good as the real thing!

Directions

CAUTION

Serrated knives are very sharp! Be really careful, or ask an adult to help you cut—especially when the bread is hot!

1 Make sure the oven rack is in the center position and preheat the oven to 350°F.

2 Line a large baking sheet with aluminum foil.

3 Using a serrated bread knife, carefully cut the bread in half lengthwise. Lay the two halves of the bread cut side up on the lined baking sheet.

STEP 3

4 Place the butter in a mixing bowl. Add the remaining ingredients and stir together with a spatula.

5 Spread the butter mixture evenly onto the cut sides of each loaf half.

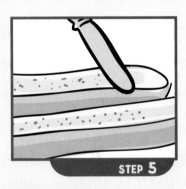
STEP 5

6 Place in the oven and bake until golden brown and bubbly, about 15 to 18 minutes.

7 Using oven mitts or pot holders, remove the sheet from the oven.

8 Carefully slice the bread diagonally and serve immediately.

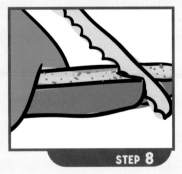
STEP 8

A garlic press is a wonderful tool—you end up with very tiny pieces of fresh garlic without your even using a knife!

BIG-BOY PIZZAS

These pizzas are the real thing, for big boys and girls who want to make their own pizza dough. You're not gonna believe how easy this is! I'm a big fan not only of cheese pizzas, like the ones we make here, but also of sausage and pepperoni pizzas. By the way, when I make meat pizzas, I do things a little different from other folks. Instead of putting the meat on top of the cheese, I put mine underneath it.

Yield
TWO 12-INCH PIZZAS

Ingredients

BASIC PIZZA DOUGH

1 PACKAGE ACTIVE DRY YEAST

1 CUP WARM WATER (110°F ON AN INSTANT-READ THERMOMETER)

3 CUPS ALL-PURPOSE FLOUR, PLUS MORE AS NEEDED FOR KNEADING

2 TABLESPOONS EXTRA VIRGIN OLIVE OIL

1 1/2 TEASPOONS SALT

Tools

MEASURING CUPS AND SPOONS, CUTTING BOARD, KNIFE, GRATER, LARGE MIXING BOWL, LONG-HANDLED WOODEN SPOON, DISH TOWEL OR PLASTIC WRAP, 2 LARGE ROUND BAKING SHEETS, ROLLING PIN (OPTIONAL), OVEN MITTS OR POT HOLDERS, SHARP KNIFE OR PIZZA CUTTER

Directions

CAUTION

1 Place the yeast in a large mixing bowl. Add the water and stir with a long-handled wooden spoon until the yeast is dissolved. After a few minutes you should see bubbles appear on the surface of the yeast mixture—this will let you know that the yeast is working. Add the flour, 1 tablespoon of the oil, and the salt, and stir well to combine. Continue stirring until the dough leaves the sides of the bowl and comes together.

2 Place the dough on a lightly floured surface. Knead until it forms a smooth, elastic ball, about 3 to 5 minutes (see page 26).

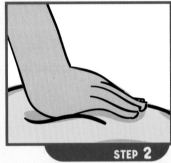

3 Grease a large bowl with 1 teaspoon of the remaining oil. Place the dough in the bowl, turning it to coat with the oil. Cover with a damp dish towel or plastic wrap. Place in a warm, draft-free place and let rise until doubled in size, about 1 to 2 hours.

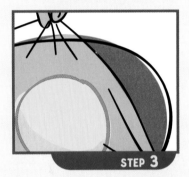

4 Place the oven rack in the lowest position in the oven and preheat the oven to 500°F.

5 Lightly grease the baking sheets with 1 teaspoon each of the remaining oil. Set aside.

6 Divide the dough into 2 portions and shape into 2 smooth balls. Pat 1 dough ball down into a flat round, about 6 inches in diameter, on a prepared baking sheet. Repeat with the second ball of dough and let both rest for 10 minutes.

7 With your fingertips, push out each dough round into a thin 12-inch round, or roll with a rolling pin (page 25).

MARGHERITA PIZZA

Ingredients

½ CUP **BEST BASIC
RED SAUCE** (PAGE
70) OR STORE-
BOUGHT
PIZZA SAUCE

4 OUNCES GRATED
MOZZARELLA CHEESE
(ABOUT 1 CUP)

¼ CUP MINCED
FRESH, CLEANED
BASIL (OPTIONAL)

1 Spoon the Best Basic Red Sauce or pizza sauce onto the dough round, and spread it to within 1 inch of the edge with the back of the spoon. Sprinkle the basil (if using) and cheese evenly on top.

STEP **1**

2 Bake on the lowest rack of the oven until the cheese is bubbly and golden brown, about 10 to 12 minutes.

3 Using oven mitts or pot holders, remove the sheet from the oven.

4 Cut the pizza into slices with a sharp knife or pizza cutter.

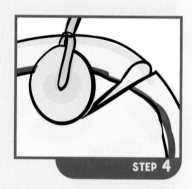

STEP **4**

THREE-CHEESE PIZZA

Ingredients

½ cup BEST BASIC RED SAUCE (PAGE 70) OR STORE-BOUGHT PIZZA SAUCE

2 OUNCES GRATED MOZZARELLA CHEESE (ABOUT ½ CUP)

2 OUNCES GRATED MONTEREY JACK CHEESE (ABOUT ½ CUP)

2 OUNCES GRATED PARMESAN CHEESE (ABOUT ½ CUP)

1. Spoon the Best Basic Red Sauce or pizza sauce onto the dough round and spread it to within 1 inch of the edge with the back of the spoon.

2. Sprinkle the cheeses evenly over the top.

3. Follow steps 2, 3, and 4 as for Margherita Pizza.

OPTIONAL PIZZA ACCOMPANIMENTS

Sliced pepperoni	Sliced or chopped onions
Cooked sausage	Sliced or chopped bell peppers
Sliced mushrooms	Different kinds of cheese

EAT-A-PITA PIZZAS

When you're not in the mood or don't have the time to make your own pizza dough, try making some Eat-a-Pita Pizzas for a quick snack or dinner. Feel free to be creative, and kick yours up with anything else you might have around, such as thinly sliced mushrooms, pepperoni slices, or even two or three different cheeses. Have fun, experiment—it's up to you! Make your pita pizzas as unique as you are!

Yield
6 SERVINGS

Ingredients
1 (1-POUND) PACKAGE OF LARGE PITA BREADS (6 PITA ROUNDS)

1 1/2 CUPS BEST BASIC RED SAUCE (PAGE 70) OR STORE-BOUGHT PIZZA SAUCE

1 1/2 CUPS GRATED MOZZARELLA OR MONTEREY JACK CHEESE (ABOUT 6 OUNCES)

Tools
MEASURING CUPS, GRATER, 2 LARGE BAKING SHEETS, OVEN MITTS OR POT HOLDERS, SHARP KNIFE OR PIZZA CUTTER, TURNER

Directions

1 Make sure the oven rack is in the lower third of the oven and preheat the oven to 400°F.

2 Lay the pita rounds on 2 large baking sheets.

3 Pour ¼ cup of the Best Basic Red Sauce or pizza sauce on each round and spread it evenly with the back of the spoon. Top each with ¼ cup of the grated cheese.

4 Bake until the cheese is bubbly and golden brown, about 6 to 8 minutes.

5 Using oven mitts or pot holders, remove the sheets from the oven.

6 Cut each pita pizza into 6 slices with a sharp knife or pizza cutter, transfer them to a plate using a turner, and serve immediately.

EAT-A-PITA PIZZA FOR ONE:
For each pita round, you'll need just ¼ cup of the Best Basic Red Sauce (page 70) or your favorite store-bought pizza sauce and ¼ cup of your favorite grated cheese. Preheat a toaster oven to 400°F and assemble your pita pizza according to the directions above. Carefully place your pita pizza in the toaster oven and bake it for 6 to 8 minutes, until the cheese is bubbly and golden brown. Using a turner, carefully transfer your pita pizza to a cutting board and cut it into 6 slices with a sharp knife or pizza cutter. Transfer the pita pizza to a plate and serve immediately.

LITTLE LAUREN'S MAC AND CHEESE

Yield

6 TO 8 SERVINGS

Ingredients

2 TEASPOONS SALT

1 TEASPOON OLIVE OIL

½ POUND ELBOW MACARONI

9 TABLESPOONS (1 STICK PLUS 1 TABLESPOON) UNSALTED BUTTER

½ CUP ALL-PURPOSE FLOUR

3 CUPS WHOLE MILK

¼ TEASPOON GROUND WHITE OR BLACK PEPPER

3 CUPS GRATED CHEDDAR CHEESE (ABOUT 8 OUNCES)

½ CUP FINE BREAD CRUMBS

2 TEASPOONS BABY BAM (PAGE 234)

Tools

MEASURING CUPS AND SPOONS, 5- TO 6-QUART POT, LONG-HANDLED FORK OR SPOON, OVEN MITTS OR POT HOLDERS, COLANDER, GRATER, 2-QUART CASSEROLE DISH, 3-QUART SAUCEPAN, WOODEN SPOON, WIRE WHISK, MIXING BOWL

Little Lauren doesn't like a lot of stuff, but she loves to make this with her daddy and then eat lots and lots of these noodles. Her father helps her with cooking the noodles and heating the oven, so she is safe. Every time they make this together, Lauren is happy-happy because this mac and cheese is really creamy and cheesy!

Directions

CAUTION

1. Make sure the oven rack is in the center position and preheat the oven to 350°F.

2. Bring a large pot of water to a rolling boil over high heat. Add 1 teaspoon of the salt, the oil, and macaroni, and stir to combine.

3. Reduce the heat to medium and cook 10 minutes, stirring occasionally with a long-handled fork or spoon to prevent the macaroni from sticking together.

4. Using oven mitts or pot holders, remove the pot from the flame and drain the pasta in a colander set in the sink, pouring away from you. Rinse under cold running water and set aside to drain well.

STEP 4

5. Grease a 2-quart casserole dish with 1 tablespoon of the butter. Set aside.

6. Melt the remaining stick of butter in a heavy saucepan over medium heat. Add the flour and cook over medium heat, stirring constantly with a wooden spoon, for 3 to 4 minutes. Do not allow the flour to brown. Using the whisk, add the milk and cook, whisking constantly, until the mixture is thick and smooth, about 4 minutes. Remove from the heat. Add the remaining 1 teaspoon of salt, the pepper, and 2 cups of the cheese, and stir well.

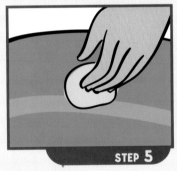

STEP 5

7. In a mixing bowl, combine the remaining 1 cup of cheese with the bread crumbs and Baby Bam.

8. Add the macaroni to the pot with the milk and cheese. Stir to combine well, then pour the mixture into the buttered casserole. Top with the seasoned cheese mixture.

9. Bake until golden brown and bubbly, about 25 minutes.

STEP 8

10. Using oven mitts or pot holders, remove the dish from the oven and let it rest for 5 minutes before serving.

SUPER STUFFED SHELLS

Yield
18 TO 20 STUFFED SHELLS, SERVING ABOUT 6

Ingredients

½ (12-OUNCE) BOX JUMBO PASTA SHELLS (18–20 SHELLS)

2 TEASPOONS SALT

1 (10-OUNCE) PACKAGE FROZEN SPINACH, THAWED ACCORDING TO PACKAGE DIRECTIONS

1 TABLESPOON PLUS 1 TEASPOON OLIVE OIL

2 CUPS FINELY CHOPPED ONION

2 TEASPOONS MINCED GARLIC

1 (15-OUNCE) CONTAINER RICOTTA CHEESE

2 LARGE EGGS

1 CUP GRATED PARMESAN CHEESE

2 CUPS GRATED MOZZARELLA CHEESE

1 TABLESPOON EXTRA-VIRGIN OLIVE OIL

1 TEASPOON BABY BAM (PAGE 234)

1 TEASPOON DRIED BASIL

1 TEASPOON DRIED OREGANO

½ TEASPOON GROUND BLACK PEPPER

3 CUPS BEST BASIC RED SAUCE (PAGE 70) OR STORE-BOUGHT PASTA SAUCE

Tools

MEASURING CUPS AND SPOONS, CUTTING BOARD, KNIFE, GARLIC PRESS (OPTIONAL), GRATER, 3-QUART POT, LONG-HANDLED FORK OR SPOON, OVEN MITTS OR POT HOLDERS, COLANDER, LARGE MIXING BOWL, MEDIUM SKILLET, LARGE SPOON

Now, a lot of you kids might think you don't like spinach, but I'll tell you what: Here's a recipe you're going to love! These pasta shells are stuffed with a delicious mixture of cheeses and spinach, then topped with our Best Basic Red Sauce and baked in the oven till hot and bubbly. Oh yeah, baby! I'm getting hungry for some of this myself, just telling you about it.

Directions

CAUTION

1. Make sure the oven rack is in the center position and preheat the oven to 350°F.

2. Bring a medium pot of water to a boil over high heat. Add 1 teaspoon of the salt and the pasta shells to the water. Cook until the shells are tender yet still firm (this is called "al dente"), about 10 to 12 minutes, stirring occasionally with a long-handled fork or spoon to prevent the shells from sticking together.

3 Using oven mitts or pot holders, remove the pot from the heat and drain the shells in a colander set in the sink, pouring away from you. Rinse under cold running water, shake gently, and set aside to drain.

4 Working over a large mixing bowl or the sink, squeeze the spinach in your hands to remove any excess liquid, then set it aside. (If your hands are small, you may need to do this in batches.)

5 Heat 1 tablespoon of the olive oil in a medium skillet over medium heat. Add the onions and garlic and cook, stirring, until very soft, about 7 minutes. Add the squeezed spinach and cook, stirring, for 3 minutes.

6 In a large bowl, use a large spoon to stir together the ricotta cheese, eggs, Parmesan cheese, and 1 cup of the mozzarella cheese. Add the spinach mixture, the extra-virgin olive oil, Baby Bam, the remaining 1 teaspoon of salt, the basil, oregano, and pepper, and stir to combine thoroughly.

7 Lightly grease a 2-quart casserole dish with the remaining 1 teaspoon of olive oil. Spoon about 2 tablespoons of the spinach-ricotta filling into each cooked pasta shell. Place the filled shells in the greased casserole dish.

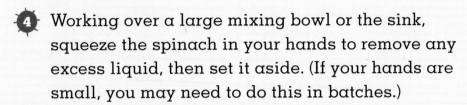

8 Pour the Best Basic Red Sauce or pasta sauce over the filled shells and top with the remaining 1 cup of mozzarella cheese.

9 Bake, uncovered, until bubbly, about 20 minutes.

10 Using the mitts or pot holders, remove from the oven and let rest for 5 minutes before serving.

WHAT'S FOR LUNCH?

CHAPTER 4

GOOD-FOR-YOU GARDEN PITA POCKETS WITH EGG SALAD

Yield
6 SERVINGS

Ingredients

EGG SALAD
6 LARGE EGGS
¼ CUP MAYONNAISE
¼ TEASPOON SALT
¼ TEASPOON PAPRIKA

PITA POCKETS
3 PITA BREAD ROUNDS, EACH ABOUT 6 INCHES IN DIAMETER
¼ CUP QUICK-AND-CREAMY HERB DRESSING (PAGE 67) OR MAYONNAISE OR STORE-BOUGHT RANCH DRESSING
1 AVOCADO
1½ CUPS EGG SALAD (ABOVE)
2 TABLESPOONS SHELLED ROASTED SUNFLOWER SEEDS

Tools
MEASURING CUPS AND SPOONS, 2- TO 3-QUART SAUCEPAN, TIMER, CUTTING BOARD, KNIFE, MEDIUM MIXING BOWL, FORK, BAKING SHEET, OVEN MITTS OR POT HOLDERS

This pita pocket, stuffed with deliciously creamy egg salad and sliced avocados, is surprisingly crunchy because it's topped with crispy sunflower seeds. Talk about something to wake up tired taste buds! Make a personal statement by choosing some of your other favorite things to go on top: Alfalfa sprouts would be my choice, but maybe you'd like some grated cheese, a sliced tomato, some crumbled crispy bacon . . . the possibilities are endless!

Directions

CAUTION

Be careful draining the hot water with the eggs—steam can burn you!

EGG SALAD

Yield ABOUT 1½ CUPS

1. Place the eggs, right out of the refrigerator, into a medium saucepan.

2. Add cold water until the water is 1 inch higher than the eggs and bring to a boil over medium-high heat.

3. Once the water comes to a boil, reduce the heat to medium-low, set a kitchen timer for 10 minutes, and cook the eggs at a low boil for exactly 10 minutes.

4. Remove the saucepan from the heat, place it in the sink, drain the hot water, and run cold water over the eggs (still in the saucepan) until they are cool enough to handle.

5. Peel the eggs.

6. Place the eggs on a cutting board. Cut each egg in half, then chop into ½-inch pieces.

7. Place in a medium mixing bowl and add the remaining ingredients, mashing with a fork to blend.

8. Serve immediately in sandwiches or cover tightly and refrigerate for up to 2 days.

STEP 6

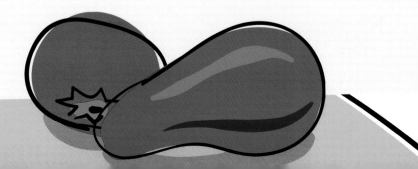

PITA POCKETS

1 Preheat a toaster oven (or regular oven with rack set in the middle) to 350°F.

2 Heat the pitas on a baking sheet until just warm and soft, about 3 minutes. Using oven mitts or pot holders, remove the baking sheet from the oven.

3 Cut each pita round in half and spread 2 teaspoons of Quick-and-Creamy Herb Dressing (or mayonnaise or ranch dressing) inside each half.

STEP 3

4 Cut the avocado into quarters lengthwise; peel and discard the pit.

5 Cut each avocado quarter into 4 slices and place 3 slices inside each pita half.

6 Spoon about ¼ cup of the egg salad into each pita half and sprinkle with 1 teaspoon of sunflower seeds.

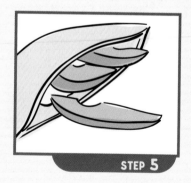

STEP 5

STEP 6

7 Add the optional ingredients, if desired, and serve.

OPTIONAL ACCOMPANIMENTS

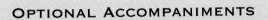

Chopped tomatoes

Minced red onion

Peeled cucumber slices

Alfalfa sprouts

Lettuce leaves

Grated cheese, such as Monterey
Jack, Muenster, or Havarti

NOTCHES-UNKNOWN PBJ

Some of the best ideas start with simple favorites. Then all you have to do is kick them up maybe half a notch or so—and BAM! You've entered another dimension! Such is the case with this sandwich. Everyone loves PBJ. But hey, add a little marshmallow cream to the equation, then cook it so that it's crispy on the outside and hot and gooey on the inside, and the results—oh, baby. Now, I'm a crunchy kind of guy myself, so I've called for crunchy peanut butter here. (Plus, the crunchy gives a nice contrast to the smooth marshmallow cream.) But if you're a creamy kind of person, no problem—just make yours with creamy peanut butter instead.

Yield
2 SERVINGS

Ingredients

3 TABLESPOONS EXTRA-CRUNCHY PEANUT BUTTER

2 TABLESPOONS STRAWBERRY PRESERVES OR OTHER JAM OR JELLY

2 TABLESPOONS MARSHMALLOW CREAM

4 SLICES SANDWICH BREAD, SUCH AS WHOLE WHEAT OR WHITE

1 TABLESPOON UNSALTED BUTTER, SOFTENED

Tools

MEASURING SPOONS, SMALL MIXING BOWL, SPOON, BUTTER KNIFE OR OTHER SPREADER, LARGE 12-INCH NONSTICK SKILLET (OR 2 SMALL NONSTICK SKILLETS), PLASTIC TURNER

Directions

1. In a small mixing bowl, combine the peanut butter, strawberry preserves (or other jam or jelly), and marshmallow cream. Stir with a spoon just until the peanut butter is swirled around with the marshmallow cream and preserves.

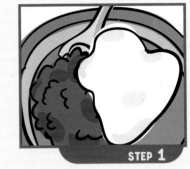
STEP 1

2. Lay 2 slices of the bread on a flat work surface.

3. Divide the peanut butter mixture between the 2 slices of bread, spread evenly, and top with remaining bread slices.

4. Spread both sides of each sandwich with the softened butter.

5. Heat a large skillet (or two small skillets) over medium-high heat, add the sandwiches to the hot skillet(s), and cook until golden on the bottom, about 2 minutes.

STEP 4

6. Turn with a turner and cook until golden on the second side, about 2 minutes.

7. Remove the sandwiches from the heat, place them on plates, cut in half, and serve.

These sandwiches don't have to be grilled, especially if you want to take one for lunch. To avoid soggy bread, try Chef Dave's freezer-fresh sandwich technique! Simply keep your sandwich bread in the freezer until frozen solid. Right before leaving for school, spread the frozen bread with the PBJ mixture. Wrap the sandwich in plastic wrap. By the time lunchtime rolls around, your sandwich will be just right for eating—not at all mushy. Chef Dave came up with this idea when he was a young boy—now he's grown-up and he works for me, overseeing all of my restaurants. You see, you're never too young to have great ideas!

Fiesta Quesadillas with Simple Salsa and Holy Guacamole

I just love quesadillas—all that gooey cheese inside a thin flour tortilla—oh yeah, baby! Make sure you kick yours up a notch or two by preparing both the Simple Salsa and Holy Guacamole to go on top. Talk about a match made in heaven!

Yield
4 SERVINGS

Ingredients
8 (6-INCH) FLOUR TORTILLAS

1 CUP GRATED MONTEREY JACK CHEESE (ABOUT 4 OUNCES)

1 CUP GRATED CHEDDAR CHEESE (ABOUT 4 OUNCES)

4 TEASPOONS FINELY CHOPPED YELLOW ONION

4 TEASPOONS VEGETABLE OIL

SIMPLE SALSA (PAGE 106)

HOLY GUACAMOLE (PAGE 107)

Tools
MEASURING CUPS AND SPOONS, CUTTING BOARD, KNIFE, GRATER, MEDIUM 8- OR 10-INCH SKILLET, TURNER, PIZZA CUTTER OR SHARP KNIFE, 2 SMALL BOWLS

Directions

1. Place 1 tortilla on a flat work surface, cover it evenly with ¼ cup of each of the cheeses, and top with 1 teaspoon of the chopped onion.

2. Cover with the second tortilla and rub ½ teaspoon of the oil onto the top tortilla.

3. Repeat this process with the remaining tortillas—you will have four stuffed tortilla "sandwiches" in all.

4. Heat a medium skillet over medium-low heat.

5. Add ½ teaspoon of the remaining oil to the pan and use a large turner to carefully transfer one of the stuffed tortillas to the hot pan, ungreased side down.

6. Cook until the bottom is just golden and the cheese is starting to melt, about 2 to 3 minutes. Gently turn with the turner and cook for about 1½ to 2 minutes, until golden brown on the second side.

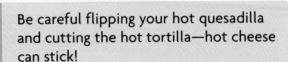
Be careful flipping your hot quesadilla and cutting the hot tortilla—hot cheese can stick!

7 Using the turner, remove the quesadilla from the pan, place on a cutting board, and slice with a pizza cutter or sharp knife.

8 Repeat with the remaining tortillas and ingredients and serve immediately with about 2 tablespoons of Simple Salsa and a dollop of Holy Guacamole.

STEP 7

SIMPLE SALSA

Yield

ABOUT 1 CUP

Ingredients

2 MEDIUM TOMATOES, HALVED AND SEEDED

½ TEASPOON SALT

½ TEASPOON MINCED GARLIC

1 TABLESPOON MINCED YELLOW ONION

1 TABLESPOON MINCED GREEN BELL PEPPER

1 TABLESPOON LIME JUICE

¼ TEASPOON EMERIL'S GREEN PEPPER SAUCE OR OTHER HOT-PEPPER SAUCE

Tools

MEASURING SPOONS, CUTTING BOARD, KNIFE, MIXING BOWL, SERVING BOWL, FORK OR SPOON

Directions

1 Place the tomato halves on a cutting board and slice into quarters.

2 Working over a mixing bowl, squeeze each piece in your hands to remove the seeds. Discard the seeds, then chop into ½-inch chunks.

3 Place the tomato pieces in a serving bowl and sprinkle with the salt. Add the remaining ingredients and mix well with a fork or spoon.

4 Let rest for at least 30 minutes before serving—this will allow the flavors to blend.

HOLY GUACAMOLE

Yield
½ TO 1 CUP

Ingredients

1 AVOCADO, PEELED, HALVED, AND SEEDED

1 TABLESPOON FRESH LIME JUICE

1 TABLESPOON MINCED YELLOW ONION

½ TEASPOON MINCED GARLIC

¼ TEASPOON BABY BAM (PAGE 234)

¼ TEASPOON SALT

¼ TEASPOON EMERIL'S GREEN PEPPER SAUCE OR OTHER HOT-PEPPER SAUCE

Tools

MEASURING SPOONS, CUTTING BOARD, KNIFE, GARLIC PRESS (OPTIONAL), MIXING BOWL, FORK, PLASTIC WRAP

Directions

1 Place an avocado half on a cutting board, flat side down.

2 Cut into sixths lengthwise, then chop into ¼-inch pieces.

3 Place the pieces in a mixing bowl.

4 Add the remaining ingredients and mash with the back of a fork until mostly smooth.

5 Stir to evenly distribute ingredients. Serve immediately or store, tightly covered, in the refrigerator for up to 1 day.

It's a BBQ Chicken Wrap, with Quick-and-Crunchy Slaw

Yield

4 SERVINGS

Ingredients

2 CUPS SHREDDED CHICKEN

2 CUPS BARBECUE SAUCE (PAGE 110) OR YOUR FAVORITE STORE-BOUGHT BARBECUE SAUCE

4 (8-INCH) FLOUR TORTILLAS

1 CUP QUICK-AND-CRUNCHY SLAW (PAGE 111)

Tools

MEASURING CUPS, LARGE MICROWAVE-PROOF BOWL, LARGE SPOON OR RUBBER SPATULA, PLASTIC WRAP, MICROWAVE OVEN, 9-INCH ROUND GLASS MICROWAVE-PROOF BAKING DISH OR LARGE PLATE, PAPER TOWEL

The sauce for this dish doesn't need to be cooked, so it's also an excellent contribution to the family barbecue when you're in a hurry. The beauty of this wrap is that you're able to use leftover cooked chicken or meat that you have on hand, from, say, a roast chicken or pork tenderloin, or even a roast beef or grilled flank steak. If you're not a coleslaw lover like I am, then just skip the Quick-and-Crunchy Slaw. Maybe you'd prefer a little grated Cheddar cheese on top of your chicken instead.

Directions

1. In a large bowl, combine the meat and barbecue sauce, and stir with a large spoon or rubber spatula to mix well.

STEP 1

2. Cover with plastic wrap and warm in the microwave for about 1½ minutes on high.

3. Place the tortillas on a round baking dish or large plate and cover with a damp paper towel. Microwave until warm and soft enough to roll, about 40 seconds on high.

4. Place one tortilla on a work surface and spread ½ cup of the meat mixture down the center. Top with ¼ cup of the Quick-and-Crunchy Slaw (page 111) and roll up into a tight cylinder.

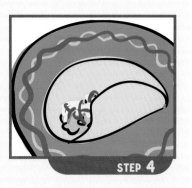

STEP 4

5. Repeat with the remaining ingredients and serve.

BARBECUE SAUCE

CAUTION

Yield

1 CUP

Ingredients

½ CUP KETCHUP

¼ CUP FINELY CHOPPED YELLOW ONION

3 TABLESPOONS LIGHT BROWN SUGAR

2 TABLESPOONS APPLE CIDER VINEGAR

1 TEASPOON DIJON MUSTARD

1 TABLESPOON WORCESTERSHIRE SAUCE

½ TEASPOON MINCED GARLIC

½ TEASPOON SALT

½ TEASPOON BABY BAM (PAGE 234)

Tools

MEASURING CUPS AND SPOONS, CUTTING BOARD, KNIFE, GARLIC PRESS (OPTIONAL), LARGE BOWL, LARGE SPOON OR RUBBER SPATULA, PLASTIC WRAP (OPTIONAL)

Directions

1. Combine all the ingredients in a large bowl and stir well with a large spoon or rubber spatula to mix.

2. Use immediately or cover with plastic wrap and refrigerate until ready to use, up to 3 days.

QUICK-AND-CRUNCHY SLAW

Yield

2½ CUPS

Ingredients

1 CUP SHREDDED
GREEN CABBAGE

1 CUP SHREDDED
RED CABBAGE

¼ CUP MINCED
YELLOW ONION

¼ CUP MAYONNAISE

2 TABLESPOONS
FINELY CHOPPED
GREEN ONION
(TOPS ONLY)

1 TABLESPOON
CREOLE MUSTARD
OR OTHER WHOLE-
GRAIN SPICY
MUSTARD

1 TEASPOON HONEY

½ TEASPOON BABY
BAM (PAGE 234)

¼ TEASPOON SALT

PINCH OF GROUND
BLACK PEPPER

Tools

MEASURING CUPS
AND SPOONS,
CUTTING BOARD,
KNIFE, LARGE BOWL,
LARGE SPOON OR
RUBBER SPATULA

Directions

1. Combine all the ingredients in a large bowl.

2. Stir well with a large spoon or rubber spatula to mix.

3. Cover and refrigerate for 1 hour before serving, or keep refrigerated for up to 1 day.

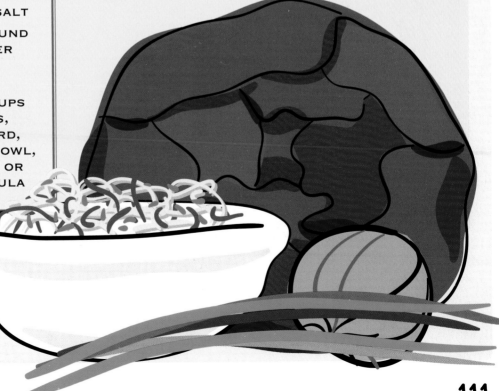

HAPPY-HAPPY CLUB SANDWICH

Yield

2 SERVINGS

Ingredients

KICKED-UP MAYONNAISE

6 TABLESPOONS MAYONNAISE

1 TABLESPOON DIJON MUSTARD

½ TEASPOON BABY BAM (PAGE 234)

SANDWICHES

6 SLICES BACON

6 SLICES SANDWICH BREAD, EACH ABOUT ½ INCH THICK

½ POACHED CHICKEN BREAST (ABOUT 6 OUNCES), SLICED, OR 6 OUNCES SLICED CHICKEN OR TURKEY

½ AVOCADO, THINLY SLICED, OPTIONAL

4 LETTUCE LEAVES

6 THIN TOMATO SLICES

Tools

MEASURING SPOONS, CUTTING BOARD, KNIFE, SMALL MIXING BOWL, FORK OR SPOON, PAPER TOWELS, 9-INCH ROUND MICROWAVE-PROOF GLASS BAKING DISH, MICROWAVE OVEN, OVEN MITTS OR POT HOLDERS, TOASTER, BUTTER KNIFE OR OTHER SPREADER, TOOTHPICKS

I've always loved club sandwiches—eating one is really like getting two sandwiches in one! And those fancy toothpicks with the different-colored plastic frills—not only do they make these sandwiches look extra special, but they also help hold all the layers together. If you can find them, go ahead and keep a supply on hand, so that anytime you feel like being at the country club, you can make yourself a Happy-Happy Club Sandwich like this one and be on your way!

Directions

CAUTION

If you don't have a microwave, make sure your parents help you cook the bacon on the stovetop—bacon splatters, and the grease could burn you!

1. Prepare the Kicked-Up Mayonnaise by combining the mayonnaise, mustard, and Baby Bam in a small mixing bowl. Mix with a fork or spoon until smooth.

2. Place two paper towels on a 9-inch round glass baking dish. Spread the bacon on the towels, slightly overlapping the slices so they fit in the dish. Cover the bacon with two more paper towels.

3. Microwave on high until the bacon is brown and crisp, about 5 minutes. Using oven mitts or pot holders, carefully remove the dish from the microwave and let it rest for 5 minutes before continuing.

4. Carefully remove and discard the top layer of paper towels. Place the cooked bacon on a plate until ready to use and discard the remaining paper towels.

5. Toast the bread until golden brown.

6. Lay the toast flat on a work surface and spread some of the Kicked-Up Mayonnaise on only one side of each slice.

STEP 6

7. Place a layer of sliced chicken on one piece of toast and top with avocado slices, if desired. Top with another piece of toast, mayonnaise side up.

STEP 7

8. On that toast, place a layer of bacon. Top with 2 lettuce leaves and 3 tomato slices.

9. Top with the remaining toast, mayonnaise side down.

10. Cut into halves or quarters. Place one toothpick into each section and serve. Let cool and eat!

STEP 8

Grill-It-Up-a-Notch Ham and Cheese Sandwich

Yield
4 SERVINGS

Ingredients

SWEET-AND-TANGY MUSTARD SPREAD

4 TEASPOONS DIJON MUSTARD

1 TABLESPOON HONEY

SANDWICHES

8 SLICES FRENCH BREAD, EACH ABOUT ½ INCH THICK

4 TABLESPOONS (½ STICK) UNSALTED BUTTER, SOFTENED

4 THIN SLICES BLACK FOREST HAM

4 OUNCES SLICED GRUYÈRE, SWISS, OR MONTEREY JACK CHEESE

Tools

MEASURING SPOONS, CUTTING BOARD, KNIFE, SMALL BOWL, FORK OR SMALL SPOON, BUTTER KNIFE OR RUBBER SPATULA, LARGE 12-INCH NONSTICK SKILLET (OR TWO SMALL NONSTICK SKILLETS), PLASTIC TURNER

This is definitely not your average run-of-the-mill grilled ham and cheese sandwich—oh, no. I start by using slices of French bread so that it gets very, very crispy. Then I smear it with some of my Sweet-and-Tangy Mustard Spread. Oh yeah, now we're talking! The mustard spread that goes on these sandwiches is also terrific with other stuff. Try it on smoked turkey sandwiches, grilled or fried shrimp, or the Twist Yourself a Pretzel we make on page 124.

Directions

1. Prepare the Sweet-and-Tangy Mustard Spread by combining the mustard and honey in a small bowl. Mix with a fork or small spoon until smooth.

2. Place all of the bread slices flat on a work surface and use a butter knife or rubber spatula to lightly spread one side of each slice with softened butter. *Use only half of the butter for this—you'll need the rest later.* (The buttered sides of the bread will go on the outside.)

3. Turn over 4 slices of bread and spread the unbuttered side with the mustard spread.

4. For each sandwich, fold one ham slice on top of the mustard spread and top with one quarter of the sliced Gruyère cheese.

STEP **4**

5. Cover with the remaining 4 bread slices, making sure that the buttered sides face out. You will have 4 sandwiches.

6. Heat a large skillet (or 2 small skillets) over medium-high heat and melt 1 tablespoon of the butter in the skillet.

7. Transfer the sandwiches to the skillet(s) with a plastic turner and cook until golden brown on the bottom, about 2 minutes.

8. Turn with the turner and add the remaining 1 tablespoon of butter to the skillet(s).

STEP **8**

9. Cook the sandwiches until the cheese has melted and the second side is golden brown, about 1½ to 2 minutes.

10. Remove the sandwiches from the pan with the turner, place on plates, cut into halves, and serve.

Ungrilled, this makes a yummy sandwich for lunchboxes. Simply prepare it as directed above (skipping the buttering and grilling steps), wrap it in plastic wrap, and refrigerate.

115

TUNA MELTS IN YOUR MOUTH

Miss Hilda used to make these on rainy days when I was a kid in Fall River, and I still love to make them when it's gray outside. To keep the bread from getting too soggy, I toast my English muffins before adding the tuna salad and cheese. If you don't have English muffins in the house, don't let that stop you from making these; just use 6 slices of whatever bread you have on hand.

Yield
3 OR 6 SERVINGS

Ingredients
3 ENGLISH MUFFINS, SPLIT IN HALF

2 CUPS TUNA SALAD (PAGE 56)

12 THIN SLICES MILD CHEDDAR CHEESE OR 6 SLICES PROCESSED AMERICAN CHEESE (ABOUT 3 OUNCES)

Tools
MEASURING CUPS AND SPOONS, TOASTER OVEN WITH A BAKING SHEET AND WIRE RACK, ALUMINUM FOIL, OVEN MITTS OR POT HOLDERS

Directions

1 Cover the toaster oven baking sheet with aluminum foil. Set aside.

2 On the wire rack of the toaster oven, lightly toast the halved English muffins—in batches, if necessary.

3 Using oven mitts or pot holders, remove the English muffins from the toaster oven and place on the covered baking sheet in one layer, cut side up.

4 Divide the tuna salad evenly among the toasted muffin halves.

5 Top each half with 2 slices of the Cheddar cheese (or 1 slice of the American cheese).

STEP **4**

STEP **5**

6 Return the baking sheet to the toaster oven and broil until the cheese is melted and bubbly, about 3 minutes.

7 Using the mitts or pot holders, remove from the oven and serve.

This tuna salad tastes just as good on regular, untoasted bread.

TOTALLY TERRIFIC CHEESE TOAST

Yield

4 TO 6 SERVINGS

Ingredients

4 TABLESPOONS (½ STICK) UNSALTED BUTTER, SOFTENED

1 ½ TEASPOONS BABY BAM (PAGE 234)

1 TEASPOON MINCED GARLIC

1 SMALL LOAF (ABOUT 10 INCHES LONG) FRENCH BREAD

⅓ POUND MILD CHEDDAR CHEESE, THINLY SLICED

Tools

MEASURING SPOONS, CUTTING BOARD, GARLIC PRESS (OPTIONAL), KNIFE, ALUMINUM FOIL, TOASTER OVEN, SMALL BOWL, SMALL WHISK OR FORK, BUTTER KNIFE, OVEN MITTS OR POT HOLDERS

This isn't just any cheese toast; this is Totally Terrific Cheese Toast the way I like it, with a little GAAAHLIC to make it extra delicious! I usually make mine in the toaster oven, and I line the bottom of the oven with aluminum foil to catch any cheesy dribbles from the toast. If you're using a regular oven, you can do the same thing, and that way cleanup is a breeze—just throw the foil away after cooking.

Directions

CAUTION

Be careful when slicing the hot loaf! Hot cheese can stick to you and burn. Have an adult help you here.

1. Place a small piece of aluminum foil on the bottom of a toaster oven and preheat to 350°F.

2. In a small bowl, mix together the butter, Baby Bam, and garlic with a small whisk or fork.

3. Split the bread in half lengthwise and spread with the seasoned butter.

4. Layer the cheese on top of the buttered bread to cover evenly.

STEP **4**

5. Bake until the cheese is bubbly and the edges are golden brown, about 8 to 10 minutes.

6. Using oven mitts or pot holders, remove the loaf from the oven and place on a cutting board.

7. Cut into 1-inch-thick slices and serve.

STEP **7**

119

CRISPY-CRUNCHY GRANOLA MUNCHIES

This not only makes a terrific snack but also doubles as an awesome breakfast cereal. Keep in mind that if you use salted nuts, you'll need to decrease the amount of salt used from a half teaspoon to a quarter teaspoon. And hey, substitute whatever nuts and dried fruits *you* like best. These Crispy-Crunchy Granola Munchies will keep up to 1 week at room temperature if stored in an airtight container—but I bet yours won't last that long!

Yield

6 GENEROUS CUPS

Ingredients

⅓ CUP HONEY

4 TABLESPOONS (½ STICK) UNSALTED BUTTER

3 CUPS OLD-FASHIONED OATS

1 CUP MIXED NUTS, INCLUDING SLIVERED ALMONDS AND COARSELY CHOPPED PECANS AND WALNUTS

½ CUP SWEETENED COCONUT FLAKES

¼ CUP HULLED GREEN PUMPKIN SEEDS

¼ CUP SUNFLOWER SEEDS

½ TEASPOON SALT

½ CUP RAISINS OR GOLDEN RAISINS (OR A COMBINATION OF BOTH)

¼ CUP DRIED CRANBERRIES OR BLUEBERRIES

¼ CUP DRIED BANANA CHIPS

Tools

MEASURING CUPS AND SPOONS, CUTTING BOARD, KNIFE, SMALL SAUCEPAN, LARGE BOWL, LARGE WOODEN SPOON, BAKING SHEET, OVEN MITTS OR POT HOLDERS, FORK, WIRE RACK, LARGE MIXING BOWL, AIRTIGHT CONTAINER

Directions

CAUTION

Be very careful when stirring the hot nut mixture!

1. Make sure the oven rack is in the center position and preheat the oven to 325°F.

2. Combine the honey and butter in a small saucepan. Heat on low heat and stir until melted. Remove from the heat.

3. Combine the oats, mixed nuts, coconut, pumpkin seeds, sunflower seeds, and salt in a large bowl. Stir with a large wooden spoon to mix well.

4. Pour the honey butter over the oat mixture and stir until well combined.

5. Spread the granola evenly in a thin layer on a baking sheet.

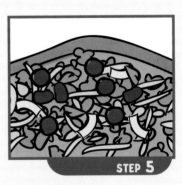
STEP 5

6. Bake, stirring every 5 minutes with a wooden spoon to prevent the granola from sticking or burning, until fragrant and golden brown, about 20 minutes. (Do not overcook—the granola will crisp as it cools.)

7. Using oven mitts or pot holders, remove the baking sheet from the oven and place on a wire rack to cool. When completely cooled, transfer the granola to a large mixing bowl and stir in the dried fruit.

8. Transfer to an airtight container and store at room temperature for up to 1 week.

An airtight container is important—this will keep your Crispy-Crunchy Granola Munchies fresh!

CRUNCHY SNACK MIX TO GO!

Yield
7 CUPS

Ingredients
8 TABLESPOONS (1 STICK) UNSALTED BUTTER

2 TABLESPOONS WORCESTERSHIRE SAUCE

3 TEASPOONS BABY BAM (PAGE 234)

1 TEASPOON GARLIC POWDER

1 ½ CUPS WHEAT CHEX CEREAL

1 ½ CUPS CORN CHEX CEREAL

1 ½ CUPS RICE CHEX CEREAL

½ CUP ROASTED PEANUTS

½ CUP CASHEWS

½ CUP ALMONDS

½ CUP PECAN PIECES

½ CUP PRETZEL STICKS

½ CUP CHEESY STAR SNACKS (PAGE 128) OR OTHER BITE-SIZE CHEESE CRACKERS

Tools
MEASURING CUPS AND SPOONS, 11 x 17 BAKING DISH OR ROASTING PAN, OVEN MITTS OR POT HOLDERS, LARGE WOODEN SPOON

Try whipping up a batch of this next time you're craving something crunchy and flavorful for a snack. Seasoned with Baby Bam, butter, and a little Worcestershire sauce, this snack mix packs a peewee punch.

Directions

Be extra careful when handling the hot baking dish!

1 Make sure the oven rack is in the center position and preheat the oven to 250°F.

2 Place the butter in a large baking dish or roasting pan and put in the oven to melt.

3 Using oven mitts or pot holders, carefully remove the baking dish from the oven and add the Worcestershire sauce, Baby Bam, and garlic powder. Stir well to combine.

4 Add the remaining ingredients and gently toss with a large wooden spoon to coat evenly.

STEP **4**

5 Return the baking dish to the oven and bake about 1 hour, until crisp and golden brown, removing from the oven every 15 minutes to stir.

6 Spread a large piece of aluminum foil on a countertop.

7 Remove the dish from the oven and spread the snack mix on the foil to cool.

8 When the snack mix is completely cool, transfer it to an airtight container until ready to serve.

Twist Yourself a Pretzel

Yield

16 PRETZELS

Ingredients

1½ CUPS WHOLE MILK

3 TABLESPOONS VEGETABLE OIL

1 PACKAGE ACTIVE DRY YEAST

2 TABLESPOONS LIGHT BROWN SUGAR

4 CUPS ALL-PURPOSE FLOUR

1 TEASPOON SALT

1 LARGE EGG

1½ TEASPOONS KOSHER SALT

Tools

MEASURING CUPS AND SPOONS, 1-QUART SAUCEPAN, INSTANT-READ THERMOMETER, 2 LARGE MIXING BOWLS, LARGE WOODEN SPOON OR RUBBER SPATULA, STANDING ELECTRIC MIXER FITTED WITH A DOUGH HOOK (OPTIONAL), SMALL MIXING BOWL, ROLLING PIN, RULER, BAKING SHEET, PASTRY BRUSH, OVEN MITTS OR POT HOLDERS, TURNER, WIRE RACK

I shape my pretzels in the traditional sort of bow shape, but you can make them into any shape you like. You can make twists, circles, or whatever strikes your fancy. If you're into dip, make a big batch of the Sweet-and-Tangy Mustard Spread that goes with my Grill-It-Up-a-Notch Ham and Cheese Sandwich (page 114).

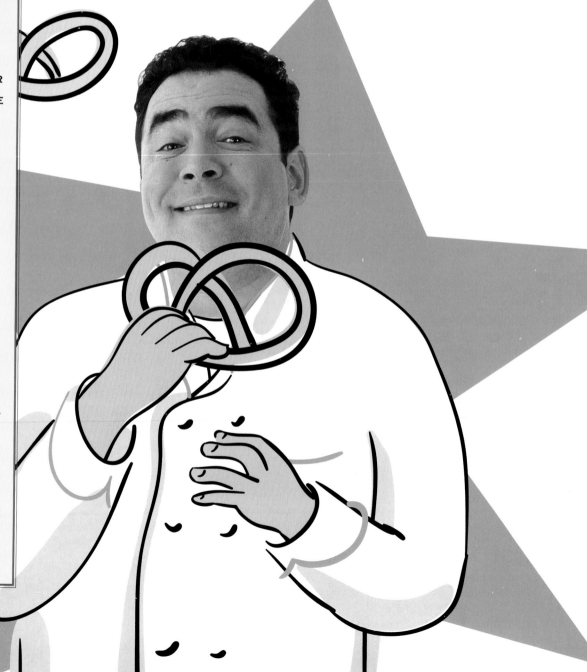

Directions

1. Place the milk in a small saucepan. Heat over medium-low heat until warm, about 110°F on an instant-read thermometer. Remove from the heat.

2. Combine 1 tablespoon of the oil with the yeast and sugar in a large mixing bowl.

3. Pour in the warm milk and stir with a large wooden spoon or rubber spatula until the yeast and sugar are dissolved. After a few minutes you should see bubbles appear on the surface of the mixture—this will let you know that the yeast is working. Let rest until slightly thickened and foamy, about 5 minutes.

4. Add the flour and the salt to the yeast mixture, stirring well with a large wooden spoon or rubber spatula until all the flour is mixed in.

STEP 5

5. Place the dough on an unfloured work surface and knead until smooth, about 3 to 5 minutes. (Or you can mix the dough in a standing electric mixer fitted with a dough hook.)

6. Grease a large mixing bowl with the remaining 2 tablespoons of oil, place the dough in the bowl, and turn to coat lightly with the oil.

7. Cover with plastic wrap and let stand in a warm, draft-free place and let rise until doubled in size, about 2 hours.

8. Make sure that the oven rack is in the center position and preheat the oven to 425°F.

9. Beat the egg in a small mixing bowl and set aside.

10. Remove the dough from the bowl and use a rolling pin to roll it out onto an unfloured surface into a 12 by 10-inch rectangle. It's good to measure with a ruler.

STEP 10

11 Cut the dough in half both vertically and horizontally, so that you end up with 4 rectangles of equal size. Repeat with each of the 4 pieces, and you'll end up with 16 equal-size pieces of dough.

12 Roll one piece between your hands and the surface to form a long, thin roll (like a snake), about ½ inch in diameter and 14 inches long. (NOTE: If the dough becomes too dry to work and will not stretch, wet your hands slightly and then try rolling it again.)

STEP 11

STEP 12

13 Bring the ends up to form a U shape and cross one end over the other at the top. Bring the ends down and across each other as though making a bow and press down on the ends to seal.

14 Place the formed pretzel on an ungreased baking sheet and repeat with the remaining pieces of dough, keeping the pretzels at least an inch apart.

STEP 13

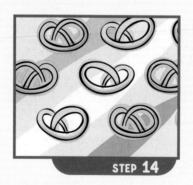

STEP 14

126

15 With a pastry brush, paint each pretzel with the beaten egg and sprinkle lightly with the kosher salt.

16 Bake until golden brown, about 20 minutes.

STEP **15**

17 Using oven mitts or pot holders, remove the baking sheet from the oven and transfer the pretzels with a turner to wire racks to cool.

18 Serve warm or at room temperature.

> If it's too difficult to make traditional pretzel shapes, try making simple twists. They taste just as good!

CHEESY STAR SNACKS

Yield

14 DOZEN 1-INCH STARS

Ingredients

1 CUP ALL-PURPOSE FLOUR

1 CUP FINELY GRATED SHARP CHEDDAR CHEESE, PACKED

2 TEASPOONS BABY BAM (PAGE 234)

1 TEASPOON SALT

½ TEASPOON DRY MUSTARD POWDER

4 TABLESPOONS (½ STICK) COLD UNSALTED BUTTER, CUT INTO ½-INCH PIECES

2 TABLESPOONS COLD WATER

1 EGG WHITE (PAGE 21)

Tools

MEASURING CUPS AND SPOONS, FINE GRATER, MIXING BOWL, 2 FORKS, PLASTIC WRAP, ROLLING PIN, 1-INCH STAR-SHAPED CUTTER, SMALL MIXING BOWL, NONSTICK BAKING SHEET, PASTRY BRUSH, OVEN MITTS OR POT HOLDERS, PLASTIC TURNER, WIRE RACKS

Here's the deal: I use a very, very small cutter for perfect cheesy bite-size snacks. It takes more time to roll out and cook these smaller ones, so if you're short on time, it's easy to either cut the recipe in half or use a larger cutter for larger stars. Or hey, make them whatever shape you like. I just happen to like stars, myself. No matter what size or shape *you* make, though, you're going to find these completely irresistible and addictive!

Directions

CAUTION

1 Combine the flour, cheese, Baby Bam, salt, and mustard in a mixing bowl.

2 Add the butter and work it in with two forks or your fingers until the mixture resembles coarse crumbs.

3 Add the cold water and continue working with your fingers until the mixture comes together to form a smooth dough.

STEP **2**

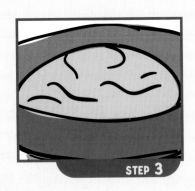

STEP **3**

4 Form the dough into a flat disk, cover with plastic wrap, and transfer to the refrigerator for at least 30 minutes and at most overnight.

5 Make sure that the oven rack is in the center position and preheat the oven to 375°F.

6 Uncover the dough, place on a lightly floured surface, and sprinkle it lightly with flour.

7 Use a lightly floured rolling pin to roll the dough out to a thickness of ⅛ inch.

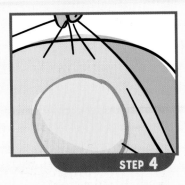

STEP **4**

STEP **7**

8. Cut the dough with a 1-inch star-shaped cutter. Gather up the leftover dough scraps, form them into a ball with damp hands, roll out as instructed in step 7, and cut into more star shapes. Repeat until all the dough has been used up.

9. Place the egg white in a small mixing bowl. Set the stars on a baking sheet and use a pastry brush to lightly paint each star with a little egg white. Bake until the stars are crisp and golden brown, about 15 minutes.

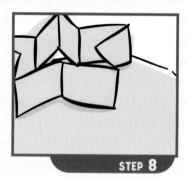

STEP 8

STEP 9

10. Using oven mitts or pot holders, remove the baking sheet from the oven and transfer the stars with a turner to wire racks to cool.

Hey, if you're up to experimenting, change this a bit by adding some dried herbs to the recipe or by using a different type of cheese. You could even toss in a teaspoon or two of Emeril's Italian Essence (or other Italian herb blend), dill seeds, mustard seeds, cumin seeds, chili powder, or garlic powder—choose the flavors that you like. Any firm cheese could be substituted, but I think that Parmesan, Swiss, or Gruyère would be delicious.

130

JILLIE'S PESTO-CHEESE DIP

Yield
6 TO 10 SERVINGS

BASIL PESTO

Yield
1 CUP

Ingredients

2 TABLESPOONS LIGHTLY TOASTED WALNUT PIECES (PAGE 233)

1 CUP CLEANED BASIL LEAVES, TIGHTLY PACKED

1 TEASPOON MINCED GARLIC

¼ CUP GRATED PARMESAN CHEESE

½ CUP OLIVE OIL

Tools

MEASURING CUPS AND SPOONS, GRATER (OPTIONAL), GARLIC PRESS (OPTIONAL), BLENDER, AIRTIGHT CONTAINER

PESTO-CHEESE DIP

Ingredients

8 OUNCES CREAM CHEESE

¼ CUP BASIL PESTO (ABOVE)

CRACKERS, BAGEL CHIPS, OR TORTILLA CHIPS

Tools

MEASURING CUPS, MICROWAVE-PROOF PLATE, MICROWAVE, OVEN MITTS OR POT HOLDERS, SPOON

My daughter Jillie came up with this recipe a couple of years ago—and talk about something totally awesome! And easy, too! Try it—you'll make your family and friends very, very happy! In case you don't already know, pesto is an Italian sauce traditionally made with a mortar and pestle, but it can be whipped up in a blender in no time at all. In Italian cooking it's most commonly tossed with pasta, but you'll find it goes really well with lots of things. Try adding a little to potato salad, drizzling it over sliced tomatoes for a fresh summer salad, or, as we do here, putting it on top of cream cheese for a tasty snack.

Directions

1 Combine all the ingredients for the Basil Pesto in a blender and process on high speed until smooth, 1 to 2 minutes.

2 Pour into an airtight container and refrigerate until ready to use, up to 3 days.

PESTO-CHEESE DIP

Directions

1 Place the cream cheese on a decorative microwave-proof plate, and microwave it, uncovered, on high until it begins to melt slightly, about 15 seconds.

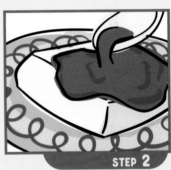

2 Using oven mitts or pot holders, remove the cream cheese from the microwave and spoon the Basil Pesto evenly over it.

3 Return plate to the microwave and cook, uncovered, on high until the pesto is just warm but still thick, 5 to 10 seconds.

4 Remove the dip from the microwave and serve with crackers or chips of your choice.

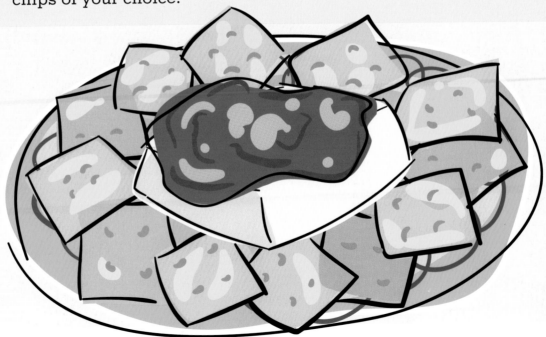

THE MAIN THING

EMERIL'S FIRST ALPHABET SOUP

Talk about the food of love! When you need something warm and soothing on a cold winter's day or you just want to do something nice for your family and friends, go ahead and make this simply scrumptious soup. It's fun to see what you can spell with the alphabet letters that end up in your bowl!

Yield
10 CUPS, SERVING 8 TO 12

Ingredients
2 TABLESPOONS VEGETABLE OIL

2 CUPS CHOPPED YELLOW ONION

1 ½ CUPS CHOPPED CELERY

1 ½ CUPS SLICED CARROTS

2 TEASPOONS BABY BAM (PAGE 234)

2 TEASPOONS MINCED GARLIC

2 QUARTS LOW-SODIUM CHICKEN BROTH

2 CUPS WATER

¼ TEASPOON GROUND BLACK PEPPER

1 BAY LEAF

1 CUP ALPHABET PASTA

Tools
MEASURING CUPS AND SPOONS, CUTTING BOARD, KNIFE, GARLIC PRESS (OPTIONAL), 5-QUART HEAVY POT, LARGE WOODEN SPOON, OVEN MITTS OR POT HOLDERS, LADLE

Directions

Remove the bay leaf before serving your soup—bay leaves are choking hazards and taste yucky on their own.

1 Heat the oil in a large, heavy pot over medium-high heat.

2 Add the onion, celery, carrots, and Baby Bam, and cook, stirring, over medium-high heat until the vegetables are soft, about 5 minutes.

3 Add the garlic and cook for 2 minutes.

4 Add the chicken stock, water, pepper, and bay leaf. Stir well and bring to a boil.

5 Reduce the heat to medium-low and simmer, uncovered, for 35 minutes.

6 Add the alphabet pasta and stir well. Simmer until the pasta is cooked through, about 10 minutes.

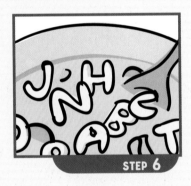

STEP 6

7 Using oven mitts or pot holders, remove the pot from the heat. Ladle the soup into bowls and serve.

You can use any small pasta shape for this soup—try orzo and stars, too!

SOME REAL GOOD CHILI

Yield

6 CUPS, SERVING ABOUT 6 TO 8

Ingredients

1 TABLESPOON VEGETABLE OIL

1½ POUNDS LEAN GROUND BEEF

2 CUPS CHOPPED YELLOW ONION

1 TABLESPOON MINCED GARLIC

2 TABLESPOONS CHILI POWDER

2 TEASPOONS BABY BAM (PAGE 234)

1 TEASPOON SALT

2 TEASPOONS GROUND CUMIN

¼ TEASPOON GROUND BLACK PEPPER

1 (15-OUNCE) CAN WHOLE PEELED TOMATOES

3 TABLESPOONS TOMATO PASTE

1 TEASPOON SUGAR

2 CUPS WATER

Tools

MEASURING CUPS AND SPOONS, CUTTING BOARD, KNIFE, GARLIC PRESS (OPTIONAL), 6-QUART HEAVY POT, LONG-HANDLED WOODEN SPOON, LARGE MIXING BOWL, CAN OPENER, OVEN MITTS OR POT HOLDERS, LADLE

Oh, baby, is this Some Real Good Chili! Try serving it in a big bowl with a piece of I-Love-Gaaahlic Bread (page 84) on the side, on top of hot dogs for a real kicked-up chili dog, as a topping for Right-Out-of-the-Oven Corn Dogs (page 160), or on a hamburger bun for homemade sloppy joes! I know a little girl named Susannah who even likes to put this on her tacos! To really kick up your chili, put a heap of shredded Cheddar cheese on top right before you serve it.

Directions

CAUTION

Be careful of splatters when cooking your meat and when bringing the chili up to a boil.

1 Heat the oil in a large, heavy pot over medium-high heat.

2 Add the meat and stir with a long-handled wooden spoon to break up the pieces. Cook, stirring, until the meat is brown and cooked through, about 5 minutes.

STEP 2

3 Add the onion, garlic, chili powder, Baby Bam, salt, cumin, and pepper, and cook, stirring, until soft, about 4 minutes.

4 Put the whole tomatoes in a large mixing bowl and squeeze them with your hands to break them into pieces.

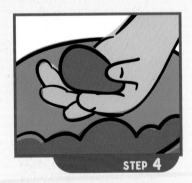

STEP 4

5 Add the squeezed tomatoes, tomato paste, sugar, and water to the pot. Stir well and bring to a boil.

6 Lower the heat to medium-low and simmer, uncovered, for 30 minutes, stirring occasionally to prevent the chili from sticking to the bottom of the pot.

7 Using oven mitts or pot holders, remove the pot from the heat, ladle the chili into bowls, and serve.

Ka-Bam Kabobs

Yield

6 SERVINGS

Ingredients

8 OUNCES BUTTON
MUSHROOMS

1 MEDIUM YELLOW
ONION, PEELED

1 LARGE GREEN OR
RED BELL PEPPER

1½ POUNDS BEEF
SIRLOIN, FAT TRIMMED
BY THE BUTCHER OR
AN ADULT

1 TABLESPOON BABY
BAM (PAGE 234)

¼ CUP
WORCESTERSHIRE
SAUCE

¼ CUP SOY SAUCE

2 TABLESPOONS
BALSAMIC VINEGAR

2 TABLESPOONS
VEGETABLE OIL

1 TABLESPOON
CHOPPED GARLIC

Tools

MEASURING CUPS AND
SPOONS, CUTTING
BOARD, KNIFE, LARGE
GLASS BOWL, DISH
TOWEL, PLASTIC WRAP,
BAKING SHEET,
ALUMINUM FOIL,
BAMBOO SKEWERS
(SOAKED IN WATER
FOR 30 MINUTES) OR
METAL KABOB
SKEWERS, OVEN MITTS
OR POT HOLDERS,
TONGS (OPTIONAL),
FORK

Kabobs are one of my favorite ways to eat beef!
Skewered with lots of different colorful veggies,
kabobs are, without a doubt, a food of love. I like to
use beef sirloin for this dish because it's tender,
and then I marinate the meat in an extra-
flavorful mixture that not only makes it taste
great but also tenderizes the meat even more.
I've given instructions for cooking these in
the oven, but if your family owns a grill,
wait for the perfect weather and cook
these outside for that serious grilled
taste. Just be sure to have your mom or
dad supervise!

Directions

C A U T I O N

Always wash your hands with lots of soap and warm water after handling raw meat!
Be careful when threading the meat onto the sharp skewers!
If you decide to grill these, do not grill without adult supervision!

1 Place the mushrooms in a large bowl of water. Gently turn them in the water to remove any grit or dirt. Quickly remove and dry the mushrooms on a clean dish towel. Set aside.

2 Cut the onion in half. Cut each half into quarters, keeping the pieces together as much as possible.

STEP **2**

3 Cut off the upper quarter of the bell pepper. Remove and discard the stem end, inside ribs, and seeds. Cut the pepper into quarters lengthwise, then into 1-inch pieces.

STEP **3**

4 Cut the meat into 1-inch pieces and place in a large glass bowl. Add the Baby Bam and toss to coat. Add the Worcestershire sauce, soy sauce, vinegar, oil, and garlic, and stir to combine. Cover the bowl tightly with plastic wrap and refrigerate for at least 2 hours and up to 4 hours.

5 Make sure the oven rack is in the top position and preheat the oven to 450°F.

6 Line the baking sheet with aluminum foil.

7 Remove the meat from the refrigerator. Carefully thread one meat cube onto a skewer, followed by a mushroom, a piece of bell pepper, and a chunk of onion. Continue threading alternating ingredients onto the skewer until it is full. Place the filled skewers on the baking sheet.

STEP **7**

8 Transfer the baking sheet to the oven and bake the kabobs for 10 minutes.

9 Using oven mitts or pot holders, remove the baking sheet from the oven. With a mitt or tongs, hold one end of a skewer. With the other hand use a fork to push the meat and vegetables from the skewer onto a plate. Repeat with the remaining skewers and serve hot.

STEP **8**

You really have to use either a glass bowl or a resealable plastic bag to marinate the meat. Metal will react with the marinade, giving the food a funny flavor.

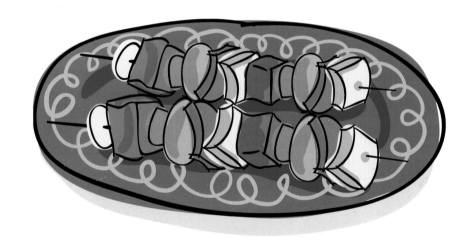

Baby Bam Burgers

There's nothing like biting into a burger and getting a mouthful of flavor, and that's what these burgers are all about. Some folks like to toast the buns lightly in the oven first, while others like theirs soft, right out of the bag. Some folks like lots of mayonnaise, mustard, tomatoes, and onions, while others prefer ketchup and pickles. Do it your way! Just make sure your meat is properly cooked. I like my burgers cooked so they are safe, and that means cooked through until they're no longer pink in the middle. They're still nice and juicy and flavorful that way.

Yield

TWELVE 2-OUNCE BURGERS

Ingredients

1 ½ POUNDS LEAN GROUND BEEF

½ CUP CHOPPED YELLOW ONION

2 TEASPOONS MINCED GARLIC

2 TABLESPOONS KETCHUP

2 TABLESPOONS SWEET PICKLE RELISH

1 TABLESPOON YELLOW MUSTARD

1 TABLESPOON BABY BAM (PAGE 234)

½ TEASPOON SALT

¼ TEASPOON GROUND BLACK PEPPER

12 HAMBURGER BUNS OR SMALL DINNER ROLLS

Tools

MEASURING CUPS AND SPOONS, CUTTING BOARD, KNIFE, GARLIC PRESS (OPTIONAL), BAKING SHEET, ALUMINUM FOIL OR WAX PAPER, LARGE MIXING BOWL, 8- TO 10-INCH NONSTICK SKILLET, PLASTIC TURNER, OVEN MITTS OR POT HOLDERS

Directions

Be careful cooking the burgers—turn them gently to avoid hot grease splatters!

1 Cover a baking sheet with aluminum foil or wax paper and wash your hands.

2 Place the meat in a large mixing bowl. Add the onion, garlic, ketchup, relish, mustard, Baby Bam, salt, and pepper, and mix with your hands until all the ingredients are well incorporated.

3 Form the meat into patties, using about ¼ cup for each. Place the formed patties on the baking sheet. Wash your hands really well with warm, soapy water before continuing.

STEP 2

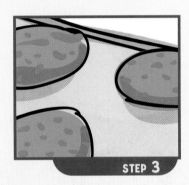

STEP 3

4 Preheat a large skillet over medium-high heat.

5 Carefully place 3 or 4 patties in the skillet, being careful not to overcrowd them. Using a plastic turner, turn the burgers over after 4 minutes. Cook the burgers on the second side for 3 minutes.

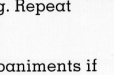

STEP 5

6 Using an oven mitt or pot holder, remove the burgers from the skillet and place on a platter or large plate while the other burgers are cooking. Repeat with the remaining patties.

7 Serve on hamburger buns, topped with accompaniments if desired.

OPTIONAL ACCOMPANIMENTS

Mayonnaise	Pickles
Mustard	Pickle relish
Ketchup	Tomato slices
Onion slices	Lettuce

LEAN MEAN TURKEY LOAF

Here's a great opportunity to get really messy and creative at the same time. And talk about terrific leftovers! To me, there's nothing like a warm sandwich made from leftover meat loaf or turkey loaf! Oh yeah, baby, now we're talkin'!

Yield

6 SERVINGS

Ingredients

1 ½ POUNDS GROUND TURKEY

½ CUP CHOPPED YELLOW ONION

½ CUP PLAIN BREAD CRUMBS

¼ CUP CHOPPED CELERY

¼ CUP CHOPPED RED OR GREEN BELL PEPPER

1 LARGE EGG

¼ CUP KETCHUP

2 TEASPOONS MINCED GARLIC

2 TEASPOONS BABY BAM (PAGE 234)

½ TEASPOON SALT

¼ TEASPOON GROUND BLACK PEPPER

Tools

MEASURING CUPS AND SPOONS, CUTTING BOARD, KNIFE, GARLIC PRESS (OPTIONAL), LARGE MIXING BOWL, 1-POUND LOAF PAN, SPOON, INSTANT-READ THERMOMETER, OVEN MITTS OR POT HOLDERS

Directions

1 Make sure the oven rack is in the center position and preheat the oven to 375°F.

2 Wash your hands and place the turkey in a large mixing bowl. Add the onion, bread crumbs, celery, bell pepper, egg, 1 tablespoon of the ketchup, the garlic, Baby Bam, salt, and ground pepper, and mix with your hands until the ingredients are well incorporated.

3 Transfer the turkey mixture to a 1-pound loaf pan and use your hands to form it into a loaf shape. Wash your hands really well with warm, soapy water before proceeding.

STEP **2**

STEP **3**

4 Pour the remaining 3 tablespoons of ketchup on the turkey and smear evenly over the top with the back of a spoon.

5 Bake until brown on top, cooked through, and an instant-read thermometer inserted into the center reaches 165°F, about 45 to 50 minutes.

6 Using oven mitts or pot holders, remove the loaf from the oven and let rest for 5 minutes before serving.

STEP **4**

You can easily make the turkey loaf into turkey burgers just by shaping them into burgers and cooking them like Baby Bam Burgers (page 144).

Man-Oh-Man Potato Casserole

Yield

8 TO 10 SERVINGS

Ingredients

1 (32-OUNCE) BAG
FROZEN TATER TOTS

4 TABLESPOONS
(½ STICK)
UNSALTED BUTTER

1 CUP CHOPPED
YELLOW ONION

1 TEASPOON SALT

¼ TEASPOON
GROUND BLACK
PEPPER

½ POUND DICED
HAM

¼ CUP
ALL-PURPOSE
FLOUR

3 CUPS WHOLE MILK

3 CUPS SHREDDED
MILD CHEDDAR
CHEESE (ABOUT
12 OUNCES)

Tools

MEASURING CUPS
AND SPOONS,
CUTTING BOARD,
KNIFE, GRATER,
9 x 13-INCH
CASSEROLE DISH,
OVEN MITTS OR POT
HOLDERS, TONGS,
4-QUART HEAVY
SAUCEPAN, LARGE
WOODEN SPOON

The first time I made this, it was for the "Kick Up Your School Cafeteria" episode on *Emeril Live*, and let me tell you, the kids at Emerson Elementary in Seymour, Indiana, went wild! I have a sneaking suspicion that you're gonna feel the same!

Directions

CAUTION

Be extra careful removing this heavy, hot, and bubbly casserole from the oven!

1 Make sure the oven rack is in the center position and preheat the oven to 425°F.

2 Place the Tater Tots in a 9 by 13-inch casserole dish and bake for 15 minutes. Using oven mitts or pot holders, carefully remove the dish from the oven and turn the Tater Tots with tongs. Return the dish to the oven and bake until crisp, about another 15 minutes. Using the mitts or pot holders, remove the dish from the oven.

STEP 2

3 Reduce the oven temperature to 375°F.

4 In a medium, heavy saucepan, melt the butter over medium heat.

5 Add the onion, salt, and pepper, and cook until soft, about 4 minutes, stirring occasionally with a large wooden spoon.

6 Incorporate the ham and cook, stirring, for 2 minutes.

7 Add the flour and cook, stirring constantly, for 2 minutes.

8 Pour in the milk and bring to a boil, stirring frequently. Reduce the heat to medium-low and simmer, stirring occasionally, for 2 minutes, or until thickened.

9 Using the mitts or pot holders, remove the saucepan from the heat and add 2 cups of the cheese. Stir until thoroughly combined.

10 Pour the milk mixture over the Tater Tots and sprinkle with the remaining 1 cup of cheese.

11 Bake in the oven until bubbly and golden brown, about 35 minutes.

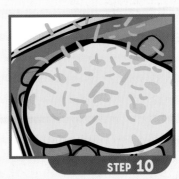

STEP 10

12 Using the mitts or pot holders, remove from the oven and let rest for 5 minutes before serving.

Yummy Creamy Chicken

Yield

ABOUT 1½ QUARTS,
SERVING 6 TO 8

Ingredients

1¼ TO 1½ POUNDS
BONELESS, SKINLESS
CHICKEN BREASTS (3 TO
4 BREAST HALVES)

1 TABLESPOON BABY BAM
(PAGE 234)

3 TABLESPOONS
VEGETABLE OIL

1 CUP CHOPPED YELLOW
ONION

1 CUP CHOPPED GREEN
BELL PEPPERS

1 CUP CHOPPED CELERY

1 CUP CHOPPED CARROTS

1 TABLESPOON MINCED
GARLIC

1 TEASPOON SALT

⅛ TEASPOON GROUND
BLACK PEPPER

½ CUP ALL-PURPOSE
FLOUR

3 CUPS LOW-SODIUM
CHICKEN BROTH

2 CUPS WHOLE MILK

1 CUP FROZEN GREEN
PEAS

Tools

MEASURING CUPS AND
SPOONS, CUTTING BOARD,
KNIFE, GARLIC PRESS
(OPTIONAL), MIXING BOWL,
5-QUART HEAVY POT,
LONG-HANDLED SPOON OR
TONGS, OVEN MITTS OR
POT HOLDERS

This dish is just that: a yummy, creamy chicken dish that can be served lots of different ways. Try yours on top of cooked white rice, pasta, or egg noodles, or even on top of split, freshly baked buttermilk biscuits. Mmmm.

Directions

1 On the cutting board, cut the chicken into 1-inch cubes. Place in a mixing bowl and toss with the Baby Bam. Wash your hands, the knife, and the cutting board well with warm, soapy water before proceeding.

2 Heat the oil until very hot but not smoking in a large, heavy pot over medium-high heat.

3 Using a long-handled spoon or tongs, carefully add the chicken and cook, stirring frequently, until browned on all sides, about 4 minutes. Add the onion, bell peppers, celery, carrots, garlic, salt, and ground pepper, and cook, stirring, until soft, about 5 minutes.

STEP **3**

4 Add the flour and cook, stirring, for 2 minutes.

5 Add the chicken broth and milk. Stir well and bring to a boil.

6 Lower the heat to medium-low and simmer, uncovered, stirring occasionally, for 10 minutes.

7 Add the peas and stir well. Simmer, stirring occasionally, for 15 minutes.

8 Using oven mitts or pot holders, remove from the heat and serve.

For a really kicked-up presentation, serve this inside some baked puff-pastry shells—you can find these in the freezer section of most supermarkets. Just follow the directions on the box and fill the pastry with some Yummy Creamy Chicken!

CHICKEN NUGGETS WITH HONEY-MUSTARD DIPPING SAUCE

Yield
4 SERVINGS

Ingredients

1 POUND BONELESS, SKINLESS CHICKEN BREASTS

3 TABLESPOONS BARBECUE SAUCE (PAGE 110) OR STORE-BOUGHT BARBECUE SAUCE

2 TEASPOONS BABY BAM (PAGE 234)

1 TEASPOON GARLIC POWDER

¼ TEASPOON SALT

3 CUPS (4 OUNCES) CORNFLAKES

Tools

MEASURING CUPS AND SPOONS, LARGE BAKING SHEET, ALUMINUM FOIL, CUTTING BOARD, KNIFE, LARGE MIXING BOWL, SPOON, LARGE RESEALABLE PLASTIC BAG, OVEN MITTS OR POT HOLDERS

Everybody's got a favorite barbecue sauce, so just use whichever one you like best for coating the chunks of chicken before tossing them with the crushed cornflakes. This recipe calls for an easy but oh-so-delicious honey-mustard sauce for dipping your chicken nuggets that would also be good with any chicken dish or even spread on a ham sandwich!

Directions

CAUTION

Salmonella warning! Always wash the knife, the cutting board, and your hands with warm, soapy water as soon as you have finished cutting up raw chicken!

1 Make sure the oven rack is in the center position and preheat the oven to 375°F.

2 Cover a large baking sheet with aluminum foil and set aside.

3 Place the chicken breasts on a cutting board and cut into 1-inch cubes. Transfer the chicken pieces to a large mixing bowl. Wash your hands, the knife, and the cutting board well with warm, soapy water before proceeding.

4 Add the barbecue sauce, Baby Bam, garlic powder, and salt to the bowl with the chicken and stir with a spoon to coat well.

5 Pour the cornflakes into a large resealable plastic bag. Let as much air out of the bag as possible, then seal it. Place it on a countertop and crush the cornflakes into small pieces with your hands by pressing down hard.

6 Place the chicken pieces in the bag with the cornflakes. Reseal the bag and toss to coat.

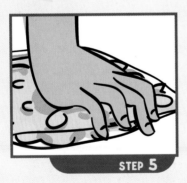
STEP 5

STEP 6

153

7 Arrange the coated chicken pieces on the prepared baking sheet. Bake until crispy and golden brown, about 18 to 20 minutes.

STEP 7

8 Using oven mitts or pot holders, remove the sheet from the oven and serve the chicken with the Honey-Mustard Dipping Sauce.

HONEY-MUSTARD DIPPING SAUCE

Yield
ABOUT ¾ CUP

Ingredients
½ CUP MAYONNAISE

2 TABLESPOONS HONEY

2 TABLESPOONS CREOLE
MUSTARD OR OTHER HOT
WHOLE-GRAIN MUSTARD

Tools
MEASURING CUPS AND
SPOONS, SMALL BOWL,
SPOON, PLASTIC WRAP

Directions

1. Put all the ingredients in a small bowl and stir well with a spoon to combine.

2. Cover tightly with plastic wrap and refrigerate until ready to use. Honey-Mustard Dipping Sauce will keep, refrigerated in a covered nonreactive container, for 2 weeks.

Some other possibilities for dipping sauces are Quick-and-Creamy Herb Dressing (page 67), Barbecue Sauce (page 110), and ketchup.

EMERILIZED TUNA CASSEROLE

Make sure you have enough potato chips on hand not only to make this recipe but also to feed the chef and any kitchen help. I don't know about you, but I always lose about half a cup of crushed potato chips to the chef's mouth during the final assembly of this kicked-up casserole! Hey, quality control is important, you know?

Yield

6 TO 8 SERVINGS

Ingredients

3 (6-OUNCE) CANS SOLID WHITE TUNA IN SPRING WATER

4 TABLESPOONS (½ STICK) PLUS 2 TEASPOONS UNSALTED BUTTER

1 (5½-OUNCE) BAG POTATO CHIPS

1 TEASPOON SALT

3 CUPS EGG NOODLES

½ CUP CHOPPED YELLOW ONION

¼ CUP CHOPPED CELERY

¼ TEASPOON GROUND BLACK PEPPER

¼ CUP ALL-PURPOSE FLOUR

3 CUPS WHOLE MILK

3 CUPS GRATED MILD CHEDDAR CHEESE (ABOUT 12 OUNCES)

1 CUP FROZEN PEAS

Tools

MEASURING CUPS AND SPOONS, CUTTING BOARD, KNIFE, CAN OPENER, GRATER, 2-QUART CASSEROLE DISH, 3- TO 4-QUART POT, LARGE WOODEN SPOON, OVEN MITTS OR POT HOLDERS, COLANDER, 4-QUART HEAVY POT, WIRE WHISK

Directions

CAUTION

1. Open the cans of tuna, drain, and set aside.

2. Lightly grease a 2-quart casserole dish with 2 teaspoons of the butter and set aside.

Be extra careful removing the hot casserole from the oven— it's not just hot, it's heavy, too!

3 Squeeze the potato chips inside their bag to break into small pieces. Set aside.

4 Make sure the oven rack is in the center position and preheat the oven to 350°F.

5 Bring a medium pot of water to a rolling boil over high heat. Add ½ teaspoon of the salt and the noodles and cook for 5 minutes, stirring occasionally with a large wooden spoon to prevent the noodles from sticking together.

6 Using oven mitts or pot holders, drain the noodles in a colander set in the sink, pouring away from you, and rinse under cold running water. Set aside and allow to drain well.

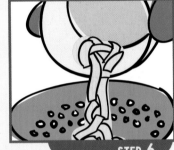

STEP **6**

7 Melt the remaining 4 tablespoons of butter in a heavy pot over medium heat. Add the onions, celery, the remaining ½ teaspoon of salt, and the pepper, and cook, stirring, until soft, about 4 minutes.

8 Add the flour and cook for 2 minutes, stirring constantly.

9 Whisk in the milk and bring to a simmer over medium-high heat, stirring occasionally. Simmer for 2 minutes. Remove from the heat.

10 Add the cheese and peas and stir well.

11 Add the cooked noodles and drained tuna and stir well.

12 Pour the tuna mixture into the greased casserole dish.

13 Top with the crushed potato chips and bake until golden brown and bubbly, about 20 minutes.

14 Using the mitts or pot holders, remove the casserole dish from the oven and let rest for 5 minutes before serving.

JUNIOR'S JAMBALAYA

Yield
8 TO 12 SERVINGS

Ingredients
1 (3½ POUND) CHICKEN, CUT INTO 8 PIECES

2 TEASPOONS SALT

½ TEASPOON GROUND BLACK PEPPER

2 TABLESPOONS VEGETABLE OIL

1 POUND SMOKED PORK SAUSAGE, CUT INTO ¼-INCH PIECES

2 CUPS CHOPPED YELLOW ONION

1 CUP CHOPPED CELERY

1 CUP CHOPPED GREEN BELL PEPPERS

1 TABLESPOON MINCED GARLIC

4 BAY LEAVES

½ TEASPOON DRIED THYME

1 CUP CHOPPED FRESH TOMATOES

3 CUPS LONG-GRAIN RICE

3½ CUPS WATER

2 CUPS LOW-SODIUM CHICKEN BROTH

Tools
MEASURING CUPS AND SPOONS, CUTTING BOARD, KNIFE, GARLIC PRESS (OPTIONAL), PAPER TOWELS, 5-QUART HEAVY POT, LONG-HANDLED TONGS, OVEN MITTS OR POT HOLDERS

The name *jambalaya* comes from the French word *jambon* (which means "ham," often found in this dish), the French phrase *à la* (which loosely translates to "in the style of"), and an African word for rice, *ya*. Jambalaya is full of flavor, easy to make, and feeds a crowd! Just make sure that you follow the steps—and don't stir until it's fully cooked!

Directions

1 Rinse the chicken pieces under cold running water and pat dry with paper towels. Place the chicken on a cutting board and season with 1 teaspoon of the salt and ¼ teaspoon of the ground pepper. Wash your hands well with warm, soapy water.

2 Heat the oil in a large, heavy pot over medium-high heat until it is hot but not smoking. Using long-handled tongs, add the chicken pieces to the pot and cook, turning occasionally with the tongs, until browned on all sides, about 8 minutes. Be very careful here—hot oil splatters!

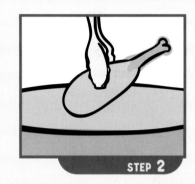

STEP **2**

3 Add the sausage and cook, stirring occasionally, until browned, about 2 minutes.

4 Add the onion, celery, bell peppers, garlic, bay leaves, thyme, the remaining 1 teaspoon of salt, and the remaining ¼ teaspoon of ground pepper, and stir well. Cook, stirring occasionally, until soft, about 6 minutes.

5 Add the tomatoes, rice, water, and chicken stock, and stir well. Bring to a boil. Reduce the heat to medium-low, cover, and simmer without stirring for 30 minutes.

6 Using oven mitts or pot holders, remove the pot from the heat and let rest. **You must let this rest, covered, for at least 10 minutes before serving. This ensures that the rice fully absorbs the liquid and is nice and fluffy.**

RIGHT-OUT-OF-THE-OVEN CORN DOGS

These are made in one of those old-fashioned corn stick pans that makes corn bread in the shape of ears of corn. By preheating the pan in the oven before adding the batter, you'll get an extra-crispy crust on the corn dogs, and they'll puff up so much, no one will ever suspect that there's a cocktail sausage inside! Now, my corn stick pan has 7 slots, but if your corn stick pan has a different number, get a grown-up to help you adjust your recipe accordingly.

Yield

7 CORN DOGS

Ingredients

3 TABLESPOONS VEGETABLE OIL

½ CUP YELLOW CORNMEAL

½ CUP ALL-PURPOSE FLOUR

1 TEASPOON BAKING POWDER

½ TEASPOON BABY BAM (PAGE 234)

¼ TEASPOON SALT

½ CUP BUTTERMILK

1 EGG

½ CUP GRATED CHEDDAR CHEESE (ABOUT 2 OUNCES)

14 COCKTAIL SAUSAGES, BOUGHT FULLY COOKED

Optional Accompaniments

KETCHUP, MUSTARD

Tools

MEASURING CUPS AND SPOONS, GRATER, CAST-IRON CORN STICK PAN, FORK, OVEN MITTS OR POT HOLDERS, SPOON, WIRE RACK, PASTRY BRUSH (OPTIONAL)

Directions

CAUTION

Be extra careful not to touch the hot pan when placing the batter and cocktail sausages in the wells!

1. Make sure the oven rack is in the center position and preheat the oven to 400°F.

2. Lightly grease the corn-shaped wells of the corn stick pan with 1 tablespoon of the oil, using either a pastry brush or your fingers. Place the pan in the oven to preheat (the pan should heat in the oven for at least 15 minutes).

STEP 2

3. While the pan is heating, put the remaining 2 tablespoons of oil, the cornmeal, flour, baking powder, Baby Bam, salt, buttermilk, egg, and cheese in a mixing bowl and stir with a fork until just combined.

4. Using oven mitts or pot holders, carefully remove the hot pan from the oven and spoon about 3 tablespoons of the batter into each well. (This will use up only half the batter.) Lay 2 cocktail sausages down in the center of each well.

STEP 4

5. Spoon the remaining batter into each well, dividing evenly among them to completely cover the sausages.

6. Bake until golden brown, about 18 minutes.

7. Using the mitts or pot holders, remove the pan from the oven and allow to rest for 3 to 5 minutes before turning the corn dogs out onto a wire rack. Serve hot, with desired condiments for dipping.

STEP 5

For a really awesome combination, try whipping up a batch of Some Real Good Chili (page 138) to serve with these—your family and friends will love you all the more!

GONE FISHIN' FISH STICKS WITH TARTAR SAUCE

Yield

4 SERVINGS

Ingredients

1 POUND BONELESS, SKINLESS FIRM FISH FILLETS, SUCH AS RED SNAPPER, COD, SCROD, OR TILAPIA

2 CUPS WHOLE MILK

2 TABLESPOONS PLUS 2 TEASPOONS BABY BAM (PAGE 234)

½ CUP DRY BREAD CRUMBS

¼ CUP FINELY GRATED PARMESAN CHEESE

Tools

MEASURING CUPS AND SPOONS, GRATER, CUTTING BOARD, KNIFE, GLASS MIXING BOWL, PLASTIC WRAP, LARGE BAKING SHEET, ALUMINUM FOIL, LARGE RESEALABLE PLASTIC BAG, OVEN MITTS OR POT HOLDERS

These fish sticks are oven-baked instead of deep-fried, for easy preparation and cleanup. Instead of using store-bought tartar sauce, why not make your own with a little mayonnaise, sweet pickle relish, whole-grain mustard, and seasonings? It's much more fun—and it'll taste better too.

Directions

1. Place the fish on a cutting board and cut into 1-inch strips.

2. Put the fish strips into a glass mixing bowl.

3. In a large measuring cup combine the milk and 2 tablespoons of the Baby Bam. Pour the milk mixture over the fish, cover with plastic wrap, and refrigerate for 1 hour.

STEP 1

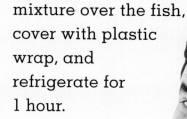

4. Make sure the oven rack is in the center position and preheat the oven to 375°F.

5. Cover a large baking sheet with aluminum foil.

6. In a large resealable plastic bag, combine the bread crumbs, Parmesan cheese, and the remaining 2 teaspoons of Baby Bam.

7. Remove the fish strips from the milk one at a time. Shake each strip to remove excess milk and drop into the bag with the bread crumbs. Toss to coat well; then place on the prepared baking sheet. Repeat with the remaining fish strips.

8. Bake until flaky and golden brown, about 20 minutes.

9. Using oven mitts or pot holders, remove the sheet from the oven and serve the fish sticks immediately with tartar sauce.

These fish sticks are also great with cocktail sauce. Try making some of your own by combining some ketchup, lemon juice, horseradish (not too much!), a little Worcestershire sauce, and maybe a drop or two of hot sauce. It's easy to make it taste the way you like it!

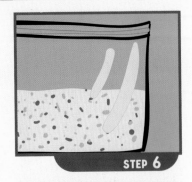

STEP 6

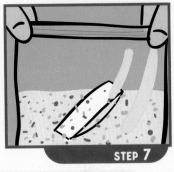

STEP 7

TARTAR SAUCE

Yield

ABOUT ¾ CUP

Ingredients

½ CUP MAYONNAISE

3 TABLESPOONS SWEET PICKLE RELISH

2 TEASPOONS LEMON JUICE

1 TEASPOON CREOLE MUSTARD OR OTHER HOT WHOLE-GRAIN MUSTARD

1 TEASPOON HONEY

½ TEASPOON SALT

Tools

MEASURING CUPS AND SPOONS, SMALL BOWL, SMALL SPOON OR FORK, PLASTIC WRAP

Directions

1. Combine all the ingredients in a small bowl and stir well with a small spoon or fork.

2. Cover the bowl with plastic wrap and refrigerate until ready to use. Tartar Sauce will keep, refrigerated in a covered nonreactive container, for up to 5 days.

163

Shake-It-Up-a-Notch Chicken

Yield
4 TO 6 SERVINGS

Ingredients
1 (3½-POUND) CHICKEN, CUT INTO 8 PIECES

MARINADE
1 CUP BUTTERMILK

2 TABLESPOONS EMERIL'S RED PEPPER SAUCE OR OTHER MILD RED-HOT SAUCE

1 TABLESPOON BABY BAM (PAGE 234)

2 TEASPOONS MINCED GARLIC

BREADING MIXTURE
2 CUPS PLAIN BREAD CRUMBS

2 TEASPOONS DRIED PARSLEY

1 TEASPOON SALT

½ TEASPOON GROUND BLACK PEPPER

1 TEASPOON DRIED BASIL

1 TEASPOON DRIED THYME

1 TEASPOON DRIED OREGANO

2 TABLESPOONS BABY BAM (PAGE 234)

Tools
MEASURING CUPS AND SPOONS, CUTTING BOARD, KNIFE, GARLIC PRESS (OPTIONAL), PAPER TOWELS, LARGE HEAVY RESEALABLE PLASTIC BAGS, BAKING DISH, TONGS, LARGE NONSTICK BAKING SHEET, OVEN MITTS OR POT HOLDERS

This is as close to fried chicken as you can get without frying and with much less mess. It's much better for you too. You're not gonna believe how crispy this chicken gets, and the flavor—oh, baby. I marinate this chicken in buttermilk and spices, and that makes it extra tender and extra flavorful. Prepare this for your family one night, and they'll love you all the more, I promise!

Directions

CAUTION

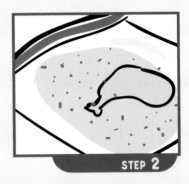

Salmonella warning! Always wash your hands well with soap and warm water after handling raw chicken!

1. Rinse the chicken pieces under cold running water, pat dry with paper towels, and place in a large, heavy resealable plastic bag. Wash your hands well with warm, soapy water before proceeding.

2. Combine the buttermilk, Emeril's Red Pepper Sauce, 1 tablespoon of the Baby Bam, and the garlic in a large measuring cup. Pour the marinade over the chicken. Seal the bag and squeeze gently so that the sauce evenly coats the chicken pieces. Place the bag inside a baking dish to prevent spills and refrigerate for at least 1 hour and up to 3 hours.

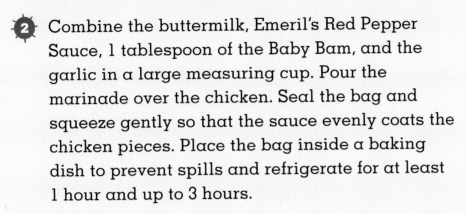

STEP 2

3. Make sure the oven rack is in the center position and preheat the oven to 375°F.

4. Combine the breading ingredients in another large heavy resealable plastic bag and shake well to blend.

5. Use tongs to remove the chicken, one piece at a time, from the marinade and drop it into the breading bag, shaking to coat well. Arrange the breaded chicken, skin side up, on a large nonstick baking sheet. Repeat with the remaining pieces.

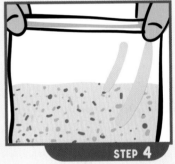

STEP 4

6. Bake in the oven until golden brown and crispy, about 45 minutes.

7. Using oven mitts or pot holders, remove the baking sheet from the oven and serve.

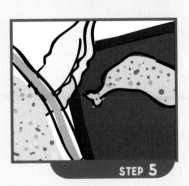

STEP 5

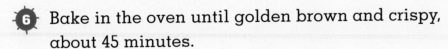

EAT YOUR VEGGIES!

CHAPTER 6

Nutty Buttery Green Beans

The toasted almonds in this recipe make these green beans extra crunchy and simply delicious—one surefire way to get those finicky friends of yours to eat their green beans!

Yield

4 TO 6 SERVINGS

Ingredients

1 POUND GREEN BEANS

5 CUPS WATER

1 1/2 TEASPOONS SALT

4 TABLESPOONS (1/2 STICK) UNSALTED BUTTER

1 (2 1/4-OUNCE) PACKAGE SLICED ALMONDS

1 TEASPOON WORCESTERSHIRE SAUCE

1/4 TEASPOON GROUND BLACK PEPPER

Tools

MEASURING CUPS AND SPOONS, 3 1/2-QUART HEAVY SAUCEPAN, OVEN MITTS OR POT HOLDERS, COLANDER

Directions

CAUTION

Be very careful when adding the green beans to the hot water—you need to do this slowly, so the water doesn't splash up and burn you.

1. Trim the green beans by snapping the ends off.

2. Place the water and 1 teaspoon of the salt in a medium, heavy saucepan and bring to a boil.

3. Carefully add the beans and return to a boil. Cook, uncovered, until tender, 5 to 7 minutes.

4. Using oven mitts or pot holders, remove the saucepan from the heat, and drain the beans in a colander set in the sink, pouring away from you. Rinse under cold running water and drain.

STEP 1

5. Melt the butter in the same 3½-quart saucepan over medium-high heat. Add the almonds, Worcestershire sauce, the remaining ½ teaspoon of salt, and the pepper. Cook, stirring, until the almonds are toasted, 2 to 3 minutes. Add the drained green beans to the pan and cook, stirring, until well coated with sauce and warmed through, about 1 minute.

6. Using an oven mitt or pot holder, remove from the heat and serve.

Did you know that toasting nuts not only makes them crunchy but also intensifies their flavor?

BROCCOLI WITH SERIOUSLY CHEESY SAUCE

I love broccoli—the way it looks
like little trees, the way it's so good for you,
and, most important, the way it tastes when you top it
with a delicious cheese sauce like the one here!

Yield
4 SERVINGS

Ingredients

1 LARGE BUNCH
BROCCOLI (ABOUT
1 ½ POUNDS)

2 TEASPOONS SALT

4 TABLESPOONS
(½ STICK)
UNSALTED BUTTER

¼ TEASPOON
GROUND BLACK
PEPPER

¼ CUP ALL-
PURPOSE FLOUR

3 CUPS WHOLE MILK

2 CUPS GRATED
MILD CHEDDAR
CHEESE (ABOUT
8 OUNCES)

Tools

MEASURING CUPS
AND SPOONS,
GRATER, CUTTING
BOARD, SHARP
KNIFE, 5- TO
6-QUART POT, OVEN
MITTS OR POT
HOLDERS,
COLANDER, TONGS,
2-QUART CASSEROLE
OR SERVING DISH,
4-QUART HEAVY
SAUCEPAN, LARGE
WOODEN SPOON,
WIRE WHISK

Directions

Be careful of hot steam when draining the broccoli—always pour away from you into the colander.

1. Place the broccoli on a cutting board and use a sharp knife to remove the tough part of the stems—usually the lower 3 to 4 inches. Cut the broccoli into 4 even portions.

2. Bring a large pot of water to a boil with 1 teaspoon of the salt. Add the broccoli and cook until tender, 7 to 8 minutes.

3. Using oven mitts or pot holders, drain the broccoli in a colander set in the sink. Use tongs to transfer the broccoli to a 2-quart casserole or serving dish.

4. In a medium, heavy saucepan, melt the butter over medium heat.

5. Add the flour, the remaining 1 teaspoon of salt, and the pepper and cook, stirring constantly with a large wooden spoon, for 2 minutes.

6. Whisk in the milk and bring the sauce to a boil, whisking occasionally. Reduce the heat to medium-low and simmer, stirring occasionally, for 2 minutes.

7. Using an oven mitt or pot holder, remove the saucepan from the heat and add the cheese. Stir well.

8. Pour the sauce over the broccoli and serve.

STEP **1**

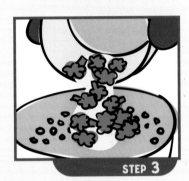

STEP **3**

This dish can easily be made ahead of time. Simply cook your broccoli and cheese sauce as instructed and combine them in the casserole dish. Once it cools, cover tightly with plastic wrap and refrigerate for up to 8 hours or overnight, then bake the dish, uncovered, in a 375°F oven for about 20 minutes, until the cheese sauce is hot and bubbly. And hey—add some chopped ham or crumbled crispy bacon to kick this up another notch! Bam!

OH-YEAH-BABY GLAZED CARROTS

I know everyone loves those tiny baby carrots that come peeled, ready to eat from the bag. So I said to myself, "Self, what about kicking those already yummy carrots up notches unknown to humankind by simply adding a little maple syrup and some butter and glazing them?" You check out the results and let me know what you think. As far as I'm concerned, I could eat a whole bag of carrots cooked this way—all by myself!

Yield
4 TO 6 SERVINGS

Ingredients
1 (1-POUND) BAG BABY CARROTS

3 TABLESPOONS UNSALTED BUTTER

¼ CUP WATER

¼ CUP MAPLE SYRUP

2 TABLESPOONS ORANGE JUICE

½ TEASPOON GROUND CINNAMON

¼ TEASPOON GROUND ALLSPICE

¼ TEASPOON SALT

Tools
MEASURING CUPS AND SPOONS, 3-QUART HEAVY SAUCEPAN, OVEN MITTS OR POT HOLDERS

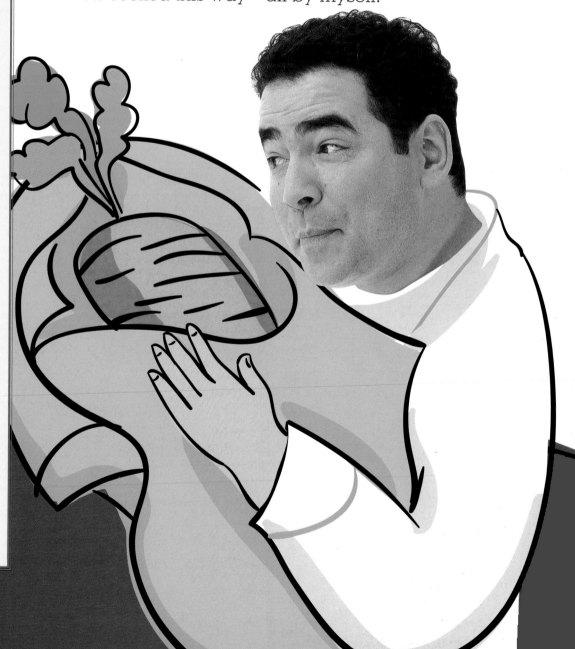

Directions

1 Place all the ingredients in a medium, heavy saucepan.

2 Bring to a boil over medium-high heat, stirring occasionally, until the carrots are tender and the sauce becomes a shiny glaze, about 15 minutes.

3 Using an oven mitt or pot holder, remove from the heat and serve.

You've probably heard that carrots are good for your eyes, but do you know why? It's because they contain high amounts of beta-carotene, a powerful antioxidant believed to have numerous health benefits. In addition to providing large doses of vitamin A, beta-carotene works with the other nutrients present in carrots to help protect against cancer, boost immune systems, and contribute to healthy hearts! Eat up!

Now-You're-Talkin' Mashed Potatoes

While there are a lot of ways to cook mashed potatoes, this is my favorite, and I happen to think it's easiest, too. And who can argue with only one dirty pot? But be careful—get a grown-up to help you while smashing the potatoes in the hot pot! Also, if you can, try to time this recipe so that you're adding the butter and milk just before you're ready to serve these—mashed potatoes are best when served right away!

Yield

6 CUPS, SERVING 6 TO 8

Ingredients

4 LARGE IDAHO POTATOES, WASHED (2½ TO 3 POUNDS)

3 TEASPOONS SALT

4 TABLESPOONS (½ STICK) UNSALTED BUTTER

¾ CUP WHOLE MILK

¼ TEASPOON GROUND BLACK PEPPER

Tools

MEASURING CUPS AND SPOONS, 4-QUART HEAVY SAUCEPAN, VEGETABLE PEELER, CUTTING BOARD, KNIFE, FORK, OVEN MITTS OR POT HOLDERS, COLANDER, POTATO MASHER OR STURDY WIRE WHISK

Directions

The potatoes need to be mashed on the stove over medium-low heat—be sure to get a grown-up to help you!

1. Fill a medium, heavy saucepan halfway with cold water and set aside.

2. Peel the potatoes. Cut one potato in half lengthwise. Place the potato half, flat side down, on the cutting board and cut each half into quarters lengthwise, so you get 4 long pieces. Holding these 4 pieces together with one hand, cut them crosswise into 1-inch cubes.

STEP 2

3. Place the potato cubes into the saucepan as they are cut, taking care to cover them with cold water—this prevents discoloration. Repeat with the remaining potatoes.

4. Once all the potatoes have been added to the pot, make sure they are covered by at least 1 inch of water. Add 2 teaspoons of the salt.

5. Bring the potatoes to a boil over high heat.

6. Reduce the heat to medium-high and continue to boil gently until the potatoes are fork-tender, about 10 minutes.

7. Carefully carry the saucepan to the sink with oven mitts or pot holders. Drain in a colander set in the sink, being careful to pour away from you.

8. Return the potatoes to the same saucepan and place it over medium heat for 1 minute.

9. Reduce the heat to medium-low and add the butter, milk, the remaining 1 teaspoon of salt, and the pepper, and mash the mixture with a potato masher or whisk until light and fluffy.

STEP 9

10. Serve immediately.

To make your mashed potatoes extra delicious try adding any of these: 1/2 cup sour cream, Baby Bam to taste, 1/2 cup chopped green onions, 1/4 cup crumbled crispy bacon, 1/2 to 1 cup grated Cheddar cheese.

Tinfoil Corn Rules!

Everybody knows how to boil corn, but try it like this for a change. It's tender, sweet, and oh-so-crunchy. It's important that you use heavy-duty aluminum foil for this recipe—it's wide enough to roll up the ears of corn really well and lock all those delicious juices inside. And hey, be careful not to burn your fingers when you unroll the corn from the foil after baking—there will be lots of steam, and it'll be really hot!

Yield

4 SERVINGS

Ingredients

4 EARS CORN

2 TABLESPOONS (¼ STICK) COLD UNSALTED BUTTER

½ TEASPOON BABY BAM (PAGE 234)

Tools

MEASURING SPOON, 4 (12 X 18-INCH) PIECES OF HEAVY-DUTY ALUMINUM FOIL, BAKING SHEET, OVEN MITTS OR POT HOLDERS

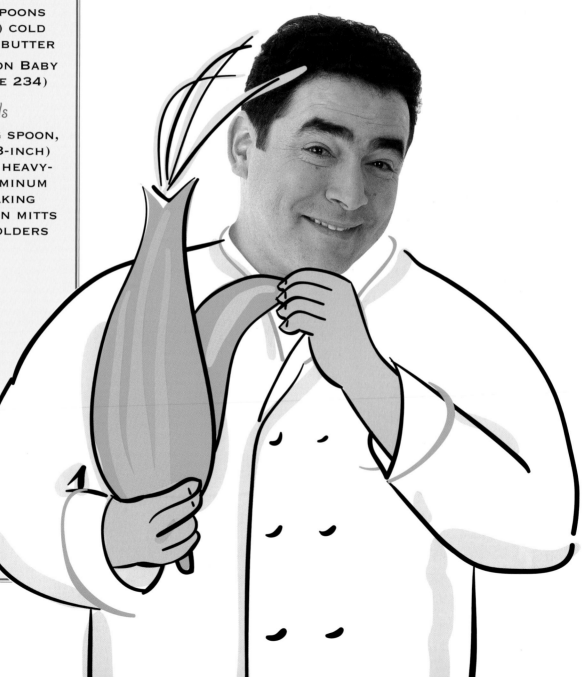

Directions

CAUTION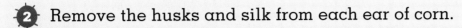

Be very careful when removing the hot corn from the foil wrapping—both the steam and the corn are hot!

1. Make sure the oven rack is in the center position and preheat the oven to 350°F.

2. Remove the husks and silk from each ear of corn.

3. Rinse the corn under cold running water and pat dry.

STEP 2

4. Cut the butter into 4 equal pieces and place one a third of the way up from the bottom on each piece of foil.

5. Set one ear of corn on top of each butter pat and sprinkle with some of the Baby Bam.

6. Roll up the foil over the corn, starting at the bottom. Keep rolling until only 4 inches of foil are left at the top, then fold the left and right sides in toward the center. Finish rolling the foil over the corn.

STEP 4

7. Place the corn on a baking sheet. Bake until tender, about 1 hour.

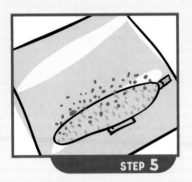

STEP 5

STEP 6

8. Using oven mitts or pot holders, remove the baking sheet from the oven and let cool for 5 minutes before taking the corn out of the hot foil.

You can try this with broccoli, cauliflower, carrots, or zucchini—but you'll have to experiment to get the cooking times just right.

177

MAKE-YOUR-OWN BAKED POTATOES WITH SPECIAL SAUCE

These baked potatoes are so large and filling, I can make dinner out of just one by itself. But if you're serving them as a side dish, you'll probably want to cut them in half lengthwise and share a potato with a friend! The Special Sauce really kicks these up!

Yield
4 TO 8 SERVINGS

Ingredients

4 LARGE IDAHO POTATOES, SCRUBBED (2½ TO 3 POUNDS)

1 TABLESPOON OLIVE OIL

½ TEASPOON SALT

¼ TEASPOON GROUND BLACK PEPPER

APPROXIMATELY ¾ CUP SPECIAL SAUCE

Tools

MEASURING CUPS AND SPOONS, CUTTING BOARD, KNIFE, BAKING SHEET, ALUMINUM FOIL, VEGETABLE BRUSH, PAPER TOWELS, FORK, OVEN MITTS OR POT HOLDERS, PLATE

178

Directions

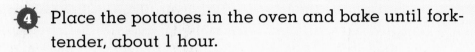

Don't pick up the hot potatoes with your bare hands!

1. Make sure the oven rack is in the center position and preheat the oven to 425°F.

2. Line a baking sheet with aluminum foil.

3. Scrub the potatoes well under running water with a vegetable brush. Dry the potatoes with a paper towel, then place them on the lined baking sheet. Using your hands, rub each potato with oil, then sprinkle on both sides with salt and pepper.

STEP 3

4. Place the potatoes in the oven and bake until fork-tender, about 1 hour.

5. Using oven mitts or pot holders, remove the baking sheet from the oven and let rest for 5 minutes. Carefully transfer the hot potatoes to a plate and serve with the Special Sauce.

SPECIAL SAUCE

Yield
ABOUT ¾ CUP

Ingredients
¾ CUP SOUR CREAM

2 TABLESPOONS CHOPPED GREEN ONIONS

1 TABLESPOON BABY BAM (PAGE 234)

Tools
MEASURING CUPS AND SPOONS, SMALL MIXING BOWL, SPOON, PLASTIC WRAP

Directions

1. In a small bowl, combine all the ingredients.

2. Stir with a spoon to blend.

3. Cover tightly with plastic wrap and refrigerate until needed, up to 2 days.

Some other kicked-up topping ideas are grated Cheddar cheese, crumbled crispy bacon, chopped ham, and cooked chopped broccoli.

MAKE-YOU-STRONG SPINACH

Yield
4 TO 6 SERVINGS

Ingredients
2 (10-OUNCE) PACKAGES FROZEN SPINACH, THAWED ACCORDING TO PACKAGE DIRECTIONS

3 TABLESPOONS UNSALTED BUTTER

1 ½ CUPS CHOPPED YELLOW ONION

1 ½ TEASPOONS MINCED GARLIC

1 TEASPOON BABY BAM (PAGE 234)

½ TEASPOON DRIED THYME

½ TEASPOON SALT

3 TABLESPOONS ALL-PURPOSE FLOUR

2 CUPS HEAVY CREAM

Tools
MEASURING CUPS AND SPOONS, CUTTING BOARD, KNIFE, MIXING BOWL, 3½-QUART HEAVY SAUCEPAN, WOODEN SPOON, OVEN MITTS OR POT HOLDERS, GARLIC PRESS (OPTIONAL)

When I was a little boy, I used to beg for canned spinach; I liked to think it would make me strong, just like Popeye! Frozen spinach is a much better alternative since it's not overcooked and still has its original bright green color from all those good-for-you vitamins and minerals naturally found in spinach. This recipe is extra rich and creamy, spinach fit for a king— so go ahead, get strong—eat your spinach!

Directions

CAUTION

1 Working over a mixing bowl or the sink, squeeze the spinach in your hands to release any excess liquid. (If your hands are really small, you may have to do this in batches.) Set aside.

STEP 1

2 Melt the butter in a medium, heavy saucepan over medium heat. Add the onions and cook, stirring, until soft, about 4 minutes.

3 Add the garlic, Baby Bam, thyme, and salt, and cook, stirring with a wooden spoon, for 2 minutes.

4 Add the spinach to the saucepan and stir to mix well. Sprinkle the flour over the spinach and stir well to combine. Cook for 2 minutes, stirring constantly.

5 Add the cream, stir well, and bring to a boil. Lower the heat to medium-low and simmer, uncovered, for 20 minutes, stirring occasionally.

6 Using an oven mitt or pot holder, remove from the heat and serve immediately.

Spinach is an excellent source of iron, potassium, and vitamins A, B₂, and C. Just a few of the many health benefits these minerals and vitamins provide are healthy blood cells, proper muscle function and fluid balance, healthy eyes and skin, stimulated immune system and speedy healing, increased energy release from food sources, and, last but not least, strong cells and blood vessels. Wow—one pretty kicked-up food source, if you ask me!

ANOTHER NOTCH FRIED RICE

Since you need cooked rice that has been cooled before making this stir-fry, this is a great way to use any leftover rice that you've already got in the fridge! Otherwise, just make the rice for this recipe a couple of hours or even the day before you plan to stir-fry it with the other ingredients. And here's something you need to remember: When making rice, don't stir it once you've covered it and lowered the heat, and don't stir it for at least 10 minutes once it's finished cooking; just let it rest. Then simply use a fork to make it nice and fluffy.

Yield

10 CUPS, SERVING 8 TO 12

Ingredients

6 CUPS COOKED BASIC RICE (PAGE 183)

4 LARGE EGGS

1 ¼ TEASPOONS SALT

⅛ TEASPOON PLUS ¼ TEASPOON GROUND BLACK PEPPER

4 TEASPOONS VEGETABLE OIL

2 CUPS CHOPPED YELLOW ONION

1 (8-OUNCE) PACKAGE BEAN SPROUTS, RINSED AND PATTED DRY

1 CUP PEELED AND GRATED CARROTS

1 CUP CHOPPED GREEN ONION

1 CUP FROZEN GREEN PEAS

½ CUP CHOPPED CELERY

1 TEASPOON MINCED GARLIC

2 TABLESPOONS SOY SAUCE

1 TABLESPOON SESAME OIL

Tools

MEASURING CUPS AND SPOONS, CUTTING BOARD, KNIFE, VEGETABLE PEELER, GRATER, GARLIC PRESS (OPTIONAL), BAKING SHEET, ALUMINUM FOIL, SMALL MIXING BOWL, WIRE WHISK, 12-INCH HEAVY NONSTICK SKILLET, PLASTIC SPOON OR RUBBER SPATULA, OVEN MITT OR POT HOLDER

Directions

CAUTION

1. Cover a baking sheet with aluminum foil.

2. Spread the cooked Basic Rice out onto the prepared baking sheet and cool at room temperature for 1 hour.

3. In a small mixing bowl, whisk together the eggs, ¼ teaspoon of the salt, and ⅛ teaspoon of the pepper.

4. Heat 2 teaspoons of the vegetable oil in a large, heavy skillet over medium heat for 2 minutes. Add the eggs and scramble, stirring constantly with a nonstick spoon or spatula. Break up the eggs into little pieces with the back of the spoon. Transfer the eggs to a bowl and set aside.

STEP 4

5 Increase the heat to medium-high and add the remaining 2 teaspoons of vegetable oil to the skillet. Add the yellow onion, bean sprouts, the remaining 1 teaspoon of salt, and the remaining ¼ teaspoon of pepper, and cook, stirring constantly, for 2 minutes.

6 Add the carrots, green onion, peas, celery, and garlic, and cook, stirring constantly, for 1 minute.

7 Add the cooled rice and cook, stirring constantly, for 4 minutes.

8 Return the scrambled eggs to the skillet and add the soy sauce and sesame oil. Cook for 2 minutes, stirring constantly.

9 Using an oven mitt or pot holder, remove from the heat and serve immediately.

BASIC RICE

Yield

6 CUPS

Ingredients

3 CUPS WATER
½ TEASPOON SALT
1½ CUPS LONG-GRAIN RICE

Tools

MEASURING CUPS AND SPOONS, 2-QUART HEAVY SAUCEPAN, FORK, OVEN MITT OR POT HOLDER

Directions

1 Place the water and salt in a medium, heavy saucepan and bring to a boil.

2 Add the rice and stir with a fork. When the water returns to a boil, cover and lower the heat to medium-low. Simmer for 20 minutes. **Do not uncover or stir while the rice is cooking!**

3 Using an oven mitt or pot holder, remove the saucepan from the heat and let the rice rest for 10 minutes before you stir or take it out of the pan.

4 Serve, or cool as directed for Another Notch Fried Rice.

Make-Lots-of-Friends Oven-Baked French Fries

You'll find that these 4 large potatoes make lots and lots of fries. If you don't have a crowd, just halve the recipe and make what you need. But be forewarned: These are addictive, and I bet you'll want to make (and eat) a lot!

Yield
6 TO 8 SERVINGS

Ingredients
4 LARGE IDAHO POTATOES (2½ TO 3 POUNDS)

3 TABLESPOONS VEGETABLE OIL

2 TABLESPOONS BABY BAM (PAGE 234)

Tools
MEASURING SPOONS, VEGETABLE BRUSH, CUTTING BOARD, KNIFE, LARGE MIXING BOWL, 2 LARGE BAKING SHEETS, OVEN MITTS OR POT HOLDERS, TONGS OR TURNER

Directions

CAUTION

1. Make sure the oven rack is in the lowest position and preheat the oven to 450°F.

2. Scrub the potatoes under running water with a vegetable brush. Pat dry.

3. Place a potato on the cutting board and cut it in half lengthwise. Place one potato half, flat side down, on the cutting board and cut each half into eighths lengthwise, so there are 8 long pieces, each about ¼ inch at the widest part. Repeat with the other potato half and the remaining potatoes. (Each potato should yield 16 wedge-shaped slices.)

STEP 3

4. Place the potatoes in a large mixing bowl and toss with the remaining ingredients.

5. Arrange the potatoes in one layer on the baking sheets.

STEP 5

6. Place the sheets in the oven and bake for 15 minutes.

7. Using oven mitts or pot holders, remove the sheets from the oven and turn the potatoes with tongs or a turner.

8. Return the sheets to the oven and bake the potatoes until golden brown, about 15 minutes.

9. Using the mitts or pot holders, remove from the oven and serve.

You don't have to peel the potatoes first. Potato peels have lots of vitamins and taste good too! Just be sure to scrub them extra well.

Sweet Potato–Praline Marshmallow Casserole

Yield

6 to 8 servings

Ingredients

2½ pounds sweet potatoes (about 3 or 4 large)

4 tablespoons (½ stick) unsalted butter, softened

2 tablespoons heavy cream

1¼ cups light brown sugar

2 tablespoons orange juice

1 teaspoon ground cinnamon

½ teaspoon allspice

⅛ teaspoon salt

⅔ cup pecan pieces

2 cups mini marshmallows

Tools

Measuring cups and spoons, 5- to 6-quart heavy pot, fork, oven mitts or pot holders, colander, cutting board, knife, large mixing bowl, large wire whisk, mixing bowl, 9-inch cake pan

Oh yeah, baby! Talk about good! This casserole is not to be missed, you've got to trust me on this one. Now, if you don't have enough elbow grease to whisk these potatoes by hand with the other ingredients, get a grown-up to help you do it with an electric mixer. The more you whisk, the smoother and lighter these potatoes will be!

Directions

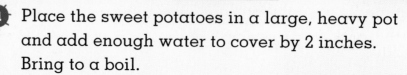

1. Place the sweet potatoes in a large, heavy pot and add enough water to cover by 2 inches. Bring to a boil.

2 Cook the potatoes at a low boil until they are fork-tender, between 30 and 45 minutes, depending on the size of the potatoes. Have an adult help you test the potatoes—the water is boiling hot!

3 Using oven mitts or pot holders, drain in a colander set in the sink, pouring away from you. Set the potatoes aside and allow to cool for at least 1 hour before handling. Be extra careful draining the potatoes—they're heavy!

4 Make sure the oven rack is in the center position and preheat the oven to 350°F.

5 Place the potatoes on a cutting board and cut in half crosswise. Gently but firmly squeeze each potato to remove the meat from the skin. Discard the skins and place the potatoes in a large mixing bowl.

6 Add 2 tablespoons of the butter, the heavy cream, ¼ cup of the brown sugar, the orange juice, cinnamon, allspice, and salt to the potatoes, and mix well with a large wire whisk until smooth.

7 In a separate bowl, combine the remaining 2 tablespoons of butter, the remaining 1 cup of brown sugar, and the pecan pieces. Stir with a fork to blend well.

8 Spoon the mashed sweet-potato mixture into a 9-inch cake pan. Dot the top evenly with the pecan mixture, then arrange the marshmallows over the nuts.

9 Bake until the marshmallows are golden brown, about 30 minutes.

10 Using the mitts or pot holders, remove the pan from the oven and let it rest for 10 minutes before serving.

IF YOU FINISH YOU CAN HAVE DESSERT!

CHAPTER 7

Big Chocolate-Chip Cookies

Yield
ABOUT TWENTY-SEVEN 4-INCH COOKIES

Ingredients
2¼ CUPS FLOUR

1 TEASPOON BAKING POWDER

½ TEASPOON BAKING SODA

½ TEASPOON SALT

1 CUP (2 STICKS) UNSALTED BUTTER, SOFTENED

¾ CUP GRANULATED SUGAR

¾ CUP LIGHT BROWN SUGAR

1 TEASPOON VANILLA EXTRACT

1 LARGE EGG, CRACKED INTO A SMALL CUP OR SAUCER

½ CUP SEMISWEET CHOCOLATE CHIPS

½ CUP MILK CHOCOLATE CHIPS

½ CUP WHITE CHOCOLATE CHIPS

1 CUP CHOPPED, TOASTED WALNUT PIECES (OPTIONAL, SEE PAGE 233 IF USING)

Tools
MEASURING CUPS AND SPOONS, MEDIUM MIXING BOWL, ELECTRIC MIXER, RUBBER SPATULA, LARGE SPOON OR PLASTIC SPATULA, TABLESPOON, 3 NONSTICK BAKING SHEETS, PLASTIC TURNER, WIRE RACKS

If you're a chocolate nut like me, these cookies are the way to go! They're chock-full of three different chocolate chips: semisweet chocolate, milk chocolate, *and* white chocolate! Oh yeah, baby—I bet you can't eat just one!

CAUTION

Directions

1. Preheat the oven to 350°F.

Be careful handling the hot baking sheets!

2 Sift together the flour, baking powder, baking soda, and salt into a medium bowl and set aside.

3 Place the butter, granulated sugar, and light brown sugar in the bowl of an electric mixer and cream the ingredients on high speed (page 24). Scrape down the sides of the bowl with a rubber spatula.

STEP 2

4 Add the vanilla and egg and mix on medium speed.

5 Add the flour mixture and mix on low speed just until batter is stiff—don't overdo it!

6 Turn off the mixer and, using a large spoon or plastic spatula, fold in the chocolate chips and the walnuts, if desired (see page 24).

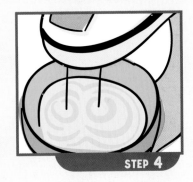

STEP 4

7 Using a tablespoon, scoop about 2 spoonfuls of the dough into a ball and place on a baking sheet. Repeat with remaining dough, keeping the scoops about 2 inches apart. Using your fingers or the back of the spoon, press down on each ball of dough to slightly flatten. You should get about 9 cookies on each sheet.

STEP 6

8 Bake until golden brown, about 20 minutes. (Depending on the size of your oven, you may need to do this in batches.)

9 Using oven mitts or pot holders, remove the cookies from the oven and transfer with a plastic turner to wire racks to cool. Repeat with the remaining sheets, if necessary.

STEP 7

It's important that you try to make the cookies about the same size, so that they're all finished baking at the same time!

MAL-MAL'S PEANUT BUTTER COOKIES

My friend Mallory Cruz and her mom make these cookies all the time for snacks and for Mallory's daddy, Tony! She usually climbs on the counter with her mom's permission and measures the ingredients by herself! Boy, are these good!

Yield

24 COOKIES

Ingredients

1 CUP CREAMY OR CRUNCHY PEANUT BUTTER

1 CUP SUGAR

1 LARGE EGG, BEATEN

Tools

MEASURING CUPS, MIXING BOWL, WOODEN SPOON, 2 NONSTICK BAKING SHEETS, FORK, OVEN MITTS OR POT HOLDERS, PLASTIC TURNER, WIRE RACK

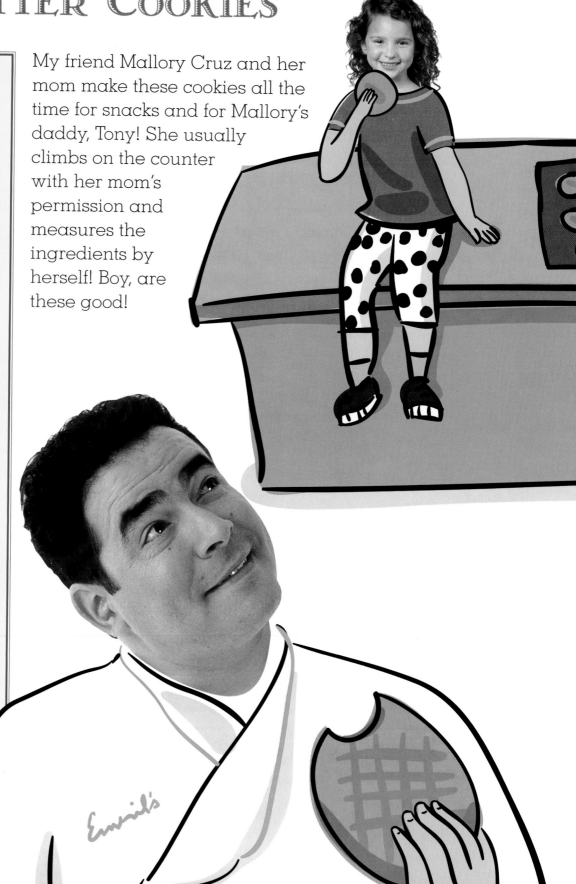

Directions

1. Make sure the oven rack is in the center position and preheat the oven to 350°F.

2. Combine all the ingredients in a mixing bowl and stir well with a wooden spoon until smooth.

3. Divide the dough into 24 portions, about 1 heaping tablespoon each.

STEP 3

4. Roll each portion between your hands to form a smooth ball.

5. Place the balls of dough about an inch apart on the ungreased baking sheets. Press down with a fork in two directions to form a crosshatch pattern. You should get 12 cookies per sheet.

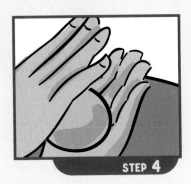

STEP 4

STEP 5

6. Bake one sheet at a time in the oven until the cookies rise and turn lightly golden, about 10 minutes.

7. Using oven mitts or pot holders, remove the cookies from the oven and let cool on the baking sheet before you lift them onto a wire rack with a plastic turner. Repeat with the remaining sheet of cookies.

BIG EM, LITTLE EM COOKIES

Yield

TWENTY-FOUR 4-INCH COOKIES

Ingredients

2¼ CUPS ALL-PURPOSE FLOUR

1 TEASPOON BAKING POWDER

½ TEASPOON BAKING SODA

½ TEASPOON SALT

1 CUP (2 STICKS) UNSALTED BUTTER, SOFTENED

¾ CUP GRANULATED SUGAR

¾ CUP LIGHT BROWN SUGAR

1 TEASPOON VANILLA EXTRACT

1 LARGE EGG, CRACKED INTO A SMALL CUP OR SAUCER

1 CUP PEANUT M&M'S

½ CUP PLAIN M&M'S

Tools

MEASURING CUPS AND SPOONS, MEDIUM MIXING BOWL, ELECTRIC MIXER, RUBBER SPATULA, LARGE SPOON, TABLESPOON, 3 LARGE NONSTICK BAKING SHEETS, OVEN MITTS OR POT HOLDERS, PLASTIC TURNER, WIRE RACKS

If you're like me, you can never really decide which M&M's you like best. So one day I asked myself, "Self, why not put both kinds of M&M's into one kicked-up cookie?" And here's the result! These cookies are going to knock your socks off, I promise! But don't try to make them any smaller—the peanut and plain M&M's need a big cookie to nest in.

Directions

1 Make sure the oven rack is in the center position and preheat the oven to 350°F.

2 Sift the flour, baking powder, baking soda, and salt into a medium mixing bowl. Set aside.

3 Place the butter, granulated sugar, and light brown sugar in the bowl of an electric mixer and cream the ingredients on high speed (page 24).

STEP 2

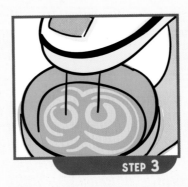

STEP 3

4 Add the vanilla and egg to the mixer and mix on medium speed.

5 Stop the mixer and scrape down the sides of the bowl with a rubber spatula (page 24). Add the flour mixture and combine on low speed. It's important to do this on low or you'll get flour all over the kitchen!

6 Stop the mixer and, using a large spoon or rubber spatula, fold in both kinds of M&M's (see page 24).

STEP 5

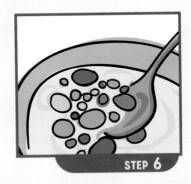

STEP 6

7 With a tablespoon, form the dough into balls, using about 2 spoonfuls for each.

STEP 7

8 Divide the balls of dough among 3 large baking sheets and press to slightly flatten, keeping the cookies about 2 inches apart. You should get 8 cookies on each sheet.

STEP 8

9 Bake in batches in the oven until golden brown, about 20 minutes.

10 Using oven mitts or pot holders, remove the cookies from the oven and transfer them with a plastic turner to wire racks to cool.

Gingerbread Friends

Yield

ABOUT FORTY-EIGHT 5-INCH COOKIES

Ingredients

½ CUP VEGETABLE SHORTENING

1 CUP LIGHT BROWN SUGAR

3 LARGE EGGS

½ CUP COLD WATER

2 TEASPOONS BAKING SODA

1 CUP MOLASSES

5½ CUPS ALL-PURPOSE FLOUR, PLUS ADDITIONAL FOR ROLLING OUT THE DOUGH

2 TEASPOONS GROUND GINGER

1 TEASPOON GROUND CINNAMON

¾ TEASPOON SALT

½ TEASPOON GROUND CLOVES

¼ TEASPOON FRESHLY GRATED NUTMEG

Tools

MEASURING CUPS AND SPOONS, STANDING ELECTRIC MIXER FITTED WITH BEATERS, SMALL MIXING BOWL, LARGE MIXING BOWL, PLASTIC WRAP, RUBBER SPATULA OR LARGE SPOON, LARGE CUTTING BOARD (OPTIONAL), ROLLING PIN, RULER, 5-INCH BOY AND GIRL COOKIE CUTTERS, 3 LARGE NONSTICK BAKING SHEETS, OVEN MITTS OR POT HOLDERS, PLASTIC TURNER, WIRE RACKS, MEDIUM MIXING BOWL, PASTRY BRUSH OR SPOON, AIRTIGHT CONTAINER

I recommend you use a standing electric mixer instead of a handheld one for this recipe, because this dough is very thick and sticky when you've finished mixing it—don't worry, this is the way it's supposed to be. That's why it needs to rest at least 4 hours or overnight in the refrigerator before you roll it out. I like to frost my cookies first, then decorate them with red hots, raisins, silver dragées (those little balls), nonpareils, sprinkles—whatever I have in my baking cabinet, really. Have fun making your gingerbread friend look like someone you know!

Directions

CAUTION

1. Place the shortening and light brown sugar in large bowl of the electric mixer and cream together on high speed (page 24).

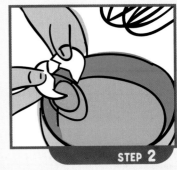

STEP 2

2. Turn off the mixer. Crack the eggs one at a time into the mixer bowl and beat well after each addition. **Be sure to turn off the mixer before cracking each egg into the bowl!**

3. In a small mixing bowl, stir together the water and baking soda. Add to the shortening and sugar mixture.

4. Add the molasses and mix well on medium speed.

5. In a large mixing bowl, sift together the 5½ cups of flour, the ginger, cinnamon, salt, cloves, and nutmeg.

STEP 5

6. Turn off the mixer, add the flour mixture to the shortening and sugar mixture, and mix on low speed until just blended. Don't overmix!

7. Place 4 large pieces of plastic wrap on a countertop. Using a rubber spatula or large spoon, divide the dough among the pieces of plastic wrap, and wrap well.

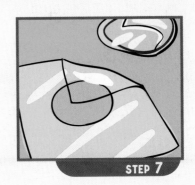

STEP 7

8. Flatten each portion with your hand and refrigerate at least 4 hours or overnight.

STEP 8

9. Make sure the oven rack is in the center position and preheat the oven to 350°F.

10. Generously sprinkle flour on a flat work surface, such as a countertop or large cutting board.

11. Take one batch of dough out of the refrigerator and place it on the floured surface. Sprinkle about 1 tablespoon of flour on top of the dough.

12. Use a floured rolling pin to roll the dough to a thickness of ¼ inch. It's best to measure with a ruler.

13. Cut out the dough with a boy- or girl-shaped cookie cutter and place the Gingerbread Friends about an inch apart on an ungreased baking sheet.

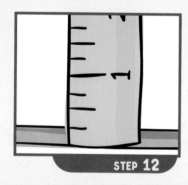

STEP 12

STEP 13

14. Form the remaining dough scraps into a ball and roll out again to ¼-inch thickness. Cut into more shapes and place on baking sheets.

15. Bake in batches until the cookies are puffed and golden— 10 minutes if you like your cookies softer, 12 minutes if you like them crunchier.

16 Using oven mitts or pot holders, remove the cookies from the oven and transfer them with a plastic turner to wire racks to cool.

17 Repeat with the remaining batches of refrigerated dough.

18 Make the glaze by combining the powdered sugar, vanilla, and milk in a medium mixing bowl and stirring well until smooth.

GLAZE

Ingredients
2 CUPS CONFECTIONERS' SUGAR

1 ½ TEASPOONS VANILLA EXTRACT

5 TABLESPOONS WHOLE MILK

19 Once the cookies have cooled slightly, frost them using a small pastry brush or the back of a spoon. Add any other desired decorations to the cookies while the icing is soft. Allow the cookies to cool completely before storing them in an airtight container.

STEP **19**

If you see your Gingerbread Friends in color, simply separate your icing into different bowls, add drops of food coloring to get the shades you want, and then frost your cookies with the colored icing. By the way, you can use any shape cutter you want. Don't limit yourself!

Real Vanilla-Bean Ice Cream

Yield

ABOUT 3½ CUPS

Ingredients

1 VANILLA BEAN

2 CUPS WHOLE MILK

1 CUP HEAVY CREAM

5 LARGE EGGS

½ CUP SUGAR

1 TEASPOON VANILLA EXTRACT

Tools

MEASURING CUPS AND SPOONS, CUTTING BOARD, SMALL SHARP KNIFE, 2-QUART HEAVY SAUCEPAN, WIRE WHISK, MIXING BOWL, LADLE, WOODEN SPOON, FINE MESH STRAINER, RUBBER SPATULA, PLASTIC WRAP, ICE-CREAM MAKER, AIRTIGHT PLASTIC CONTAINER (OPTIONAL)

I cannot tell a lie: Sometimes I do enjoy all those fancy, kicked-up ice-cream flavors—but there's nothing like the simple goodness of homemade vanilla ice cream. Great vanilla ice cream like this is always made with real vanilla beans and not only is delicious on its own but may also be a kicker-upper to just about anything you can imagine: cakes, cookies, crisps, cobblers, you name it—they all taste better with a scoop of Real Vanilla-Bean Ice Cream on top.

Directions

CAUTION

This recipe calls for a lot of hot liquid—be careful!

1 With a small sharp knife cut the vanilla bean in half lengthwise.

2 Place the milk and cream in a small, heavy saucepan. Using the tip of the knife, scrape the seeds from the vanilla bean halves into the milk and add both halves to the saucepan.

STEP **1**

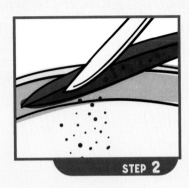

STEP **2**

3 Set the saucepan on the stovetop and bring to a simmer over medium heat. Remove from the heat.

4 Crack the eggs and whisk the eggs and sugar in a mixing bowl until pale yellow and well combined, about 2 minutes.

5 Using a ladle, add about ½ cup of the hot milk mixture to the eggs and whisk to combine.

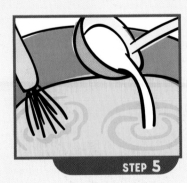

STEP **5**

6 Add the egg mixture to the hot milk in the saucepan and stir well with a wooden spoon.

7 Return the pan to medium heat and cook, stirring constantly, until the mixture is slightly thickened and coats the back of a spoon, about 5 minutes. This is called a custard.

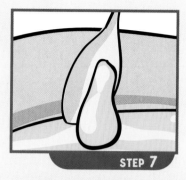
STEP 7

8 Remove the custard from the heat and strain through a fine mesh strainer into a clean mixing bowl, pressing down on the strainer with a rubber spatula to get as much liquid as possible into the bowl.

9 Discard the vanilla bean halves and any other solids sticking to the strainer.

STEP 8

10 Add the vanilla extract to the bowl. Stir the custard for 5 minutes with a whisk until cooled slightly.

11 Cover the bowl with plastic wrap, pressing the wrap gently against the surface of the custard. Refrigerate until thoroughly chilled, about 2 hours, stirring occasionally.

STEP 11

12 Pour the custard into the bowl of an ice-cream maker and process according to manufacturer's directions.

13 Serve immediately or transfer to an airtight plastic container and store in the freezer for up to 1 week.

Pressing the plastic wrap onto the surface of the custard ensures that no thick "skin" will form on the top.

Just-Like-Mom's Cupcakes with Vanilla and Chocolate Icings

Yield

16 CUPCAKES

Ingredients

CUPCAKES

1 LARGE EGG, CRACKED INTO A SMALL CUP OR SAUCER

½ CUP (1 STICK) UNSALTED BUTTER, SOFTENED

1 ½ CUPS ALL-PURPOSE FLOUR

½ CUP SIFTED COCOA POWDER
(FOR CHOCOLATE CUPCAKES)

½ CUP BUTTERMILK

1 TEASPOON VANILLA EXTRACT

1 TEASPOON BAKING SODA

½ TEASPOON SALT

1 CUP GRANULATED SUGAR

½ CUP HOT WATER

ICING

3 CUPS CONFECTIONERS' SUGAR, SIFTED

3 TABLESPOONS SIFTED COCOA POWDER
(FOR CHOCOLATE ICING)

2 TABLESPOONS WHOLE MILK

2 TABLESPOONS BUTTERMILK

4 TABLESPOONS (½ STICK) UNSALTED BUTTER,
SOFTENED

1 TEASPOON VANILLA EXTRACT

⅛ TEASPOON SALT

Tools

MEASURING CUPS AND SPOONS, 2 (12-CUP) MUFFIN TINS, 16 PAPER MUFFIN-TIN LINERS, MIXING BOWL, HANDHELD ELECTRIC MIXER, TOOTHPICKS, OVEN MITTS OR POT HOLDERS, WIRE RACK, SMALL RUBBER SPATULA OR BUTTER KNIFE, LARGE MIXING BOWL

Cupcakes are lots of fun because everyone gets to have a cake of their very own! Depending on your mood, you can make either vanilla or chocolate cupcakes using this recipe, and either vanilla or chocolate icing. The only difference is that for chocolate, you add a little sifted cocoa to each basic recipe. Easy as cake! And hey, if you want to take these to the next level, you can always dip your frosted cupcakes in chocolate sprinkles; gold or silver dragées; mini chocolate chips; blueberries; chopped nuts; or even crushed Oreos. The sky's the limit on these babies!

Directions

CAUTION

1 Make sure the oven rack is in the center position and preheat the oven to 350°F.

2 Line one 12-cup muffin tin with 12 paper muffin-tin liners and place 4 paper muffin-tin liners inside the other muffin tin. Add 2 tablespoons of water to each of the paperless muffin wells.

STEP 2

3 Place all the cupcake ingredients in a mixing bowl, adding the hot water last. Beat with an electric mixer until smooth.

4 Divide the batter evenly among the paper muffin-tin liners.

5 Bake 20 to 25 minutes, until the cupcakes rise and turn golden and a toothpick inserted into the center of one comes out clean.

6 Using oven mitts or pot holders, remove the tins from the oven and carefully transfer the cupcakes to a wire rack to cool completely. Be careful not to spill the water in the empty wells.

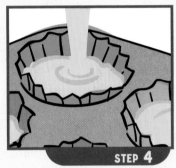
STEP 4

7 Using a small spatula or butter knife, frost each cupcake with whichever icing you've chosen to make (use about 2 tablespoons per cupcake).

ICING

Directions

1 Combine all the ingredients in a large mixing bowl.

2 Blend with a handheld mixer until smooth and creamy. The icing can be made and kept refrigerated, tightly covered, for up to 1 week.

3 Use to frost the cupcakes and serve.

If you want, place these kick-it-up toppings on separate plates and dip the frosted cupcakes into any (or all) of them before serving.

OPTIONAL ACCOMPANIMENTS

Chocolate sprinkles	M&M's
Multicolored sprinkles	Crushed Oreo cookies
Colored sugar	Fresh blueberries
Silver dragées (balls)	Toasted chopped nuts
Mini chocolate chips	

FRESH-AND-FRUITY FREEZE POPS

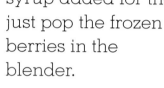

Use whatever fruits are in season and whatever fruits you like best for these treats. I make mine with strawberries, raspberries, and blueberries, but what you use is up to you! Oh, and if it's that in-between time of year and you can't get fresh berries, use frozen 100 percent natural fruits with no syrup added for the same great results; just pop the frozen berries in the blender.

Yield
4 POPS

Ingredients
1 ½ CUPS STRAWBERRIES (SLICED LENGTHWISE TO ABOUT ¼ INCH THICKNESS)

½ CUP RASPBERRIES

½ CUP BLUEBERRIES

½ CUP SIMPLE SYRUP (PAGE 232)

Tools
MEASURING CUPS, BLENDER, 4 (5-OUNCE) PAPER CUPS, 4 ICE-CREAM STICKS OR PLASTIC SPOONS, 4 (4-INCH) SQUARES OF ALUMINUM FOIL

Directions

CAUTION

Blender blades are sharp—keep your fingers away! Make sure the lid is on tight before pureeing the fruit!

1 Place all of the ingredients in a blender and puree on high speed until well blended and smooth, about 30 seconds.

2 Divide the fruit puree among 4 paper cups (about ½ cup puree per cup).

3 Stand 1 ice-cream stick or plastic spoon in the center of each cup.

STEP 2

STEP 3

4 Poke a small hole in the center of each foil square and place one square over each cup, pushing the stick or spoon handle through the hole to hold it straight.

5 Stand the cups in the freezer and freeze until set, at least 8 hours or overnight. Remove the pops from the freezer and discard the foil squares.

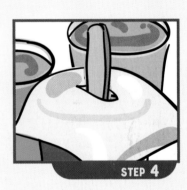
STEP 4

6 Gently tear the paper cups away from the fruit pops and serve.

Other fruit possibilities for pops are mangoes, bananas, peaches, nectarines, pineapple, and cherries. Use the fruits that *you* love.

STEP 6

Jessie's Chocolate-Dipped Strawberries

My daughter Jessie just loves strawberries fixed this way. When I first opened Emeril's Restaurant in New Orleans, she was still a little girl, and whenever she came to see me at the restaurant, I always made sure that there were some freshly dipped strawberries in the pastry kitchen, waiting for her approval!

Yield
1 PINT

Ingredients
1 PINT FRESH STRAWBERRIES WITH THE STEMS ON

1 CUP SEMISWEET OR BITTERSWEET CHOCOLATE CHIPS

Tools
MEASURING CUP, BAKING SHEET, PARCHMENT OR WAXED PAPER, MICROWAVE-PROOF GLASS BOWL OR DOUBLE BOILER

210

Directions

CAUTION

Have an adult help you melt the chocolate.
Be careful when dipping the strawberries in the hot chocolate!

1 Wash the strawberries as quickly as possible so they don't get soggy. Make sure to dry them very well before dipping them in the chocolate.

2 Line a baking sheet with parchment or waxed paper.

STEP **2**

3 Place chocolate chips in a microwave-proof glass bowl or measuring cup and cover it with plastic wrap. Microwave the chocolate on high power for 30 seconds; then stir it with a spoon or rubber spatula. Continue to microwave the chocolate on high, stopping to stir every 30 seconds, until it is completely melted and smooth. (If you don't have a microwave, you can use the double-boiler method for melting chocolate on page 26.)

4 Holding it by its stem, dip each strawberry into the melted chocolate and place them on the lined baking sheet. Place the sheet in the refrigerator and allow it to cool 10 to 15 minutes, just until the chocolate has hardened.

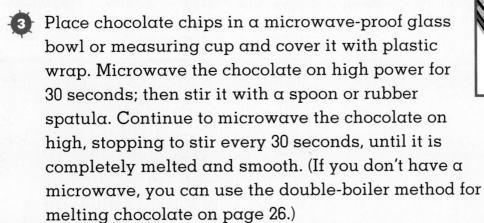

STEP **4**

MAKE-YOURSELF-SOME APPLESAUCE

I like my applesauce sweet, but not too sweet. Depending on your taste, you might find this just right. But hey, if it needs more sugar for your liking, go ahead and add more, a little bit at a time. I use red apples to make this applesauce, and I don't peel them first, so the applesauce ends up a nice pink color. You probably won't be able to eat all two and a half cups the same day you make this, so transfer your applesauce to a large, clean jar—where it will keep in the refrigerator for up to 1 week.

Yield

2½ CUPS, SERVING ABOUT 6

Ingredients

6 ROME APPLES

1 CUP WATER

1 TABLESPOON LEMON JUICE

¾ TEASPOON GROUND CINNAMON

¼ CUP SUGAR

Tools

MEASURING CUPS AND SPOONS, APPLE CORER, CUTTING BOARD, KNIFE, 3-QUART HEAVY SAUCEPAN, LARGE WOODEN OR METAL SPOON, OVEN MITT OR POT HOLDER, POTATO MASHER, COARSE METAL STRAINER, LARGE MIXING BOWL, HEAVY METAL LADLE OR SPOON

CAUTION

Directions

1. Core all 6 apples, following the directions on page 20.

STEP 1

Be careful mashing the hot apples!

2 Cut one apple in half lengthwise. Place the halves flat on the cutting board and cut each one into quarters lengthwise. Place the apple pieces in a medium, heavy saucepan. Repeat with the remaining apples.

STEP 2

3 Add the remaining ingredients to the saucepan and bring to a boil over high heat, stirring frequently with a large wooden or metal spoon.

4 Reduce the heat to medium-low, cover, and simmer, stirring occasionally, until the apples become very soft and begin to break apart.

5 Using an oven mitt or pot holder, remove the pan from the heat and mash the apples with a potato masher until smooth.

6 Spoon the apples into a coarse metal strainer set over a large mixing bowl.

STEP 5

7 Using a heavy metal ladle or spoon, press the apples against the strainer to push out as much apple puree as possible. Discard the peels.

8 Transfer the applesauce to the refrigerator until cooled, stirring frequently, about 1½ hours. Once cooled, serve the applesauce or cover it tightly and refrigerate it for up to 1 week.

STEP 7

You'll-Go-Ape for Chocolate-Covered Bananas

Yield

8 SERVINGS

Ingredients

4 BANANAS

½ CUP HEAVY CREAM

1 CUP SEMISWEET CHOCOLATE CHIPS

½ CUP LIGHTLY TOASTED COCONUT (PAGE 233) OR ½ CUP CHOPPED ROASTED PEANUTS (OR ¼ CUP OF EACH)

Tools

MEASURING CUPS, CUTTING BOARD, KNIFE, 8 ICE-CREAM STICKS OR 4 LARGE BAMBOO SKEWERS CUT IN HALF CROSSWISE, 8 (4 x 6-INCH) PIECES OF ALUMINUM FOIL, SMALL SAUCEPAN, MEDIUM MIXING BOWL, SMALL SPOON OR RUBBER SPATULA, 2 SMALL MIXING BOWLS, BAKING SHEET, WAXED PAPER, ALUMINUM FOIL

So simple and yet so good, these bananas are great treats to keep in the freezer for rainy days! I don't know which ones I like best—the ones sprinkled with toasted coconut or the ones sprinkled with chopped peanuts. They're both pretty kicked-up, if you ask me. Choose for yourself—or, make them both ways!

Directions

CAUTION

Be careful when pouring the hot cream over the chocolate chips!

1. Peel the bananas and cut them in half crosswise so that you now have 2 short pieces.

2. Insert an ice-cream stick or half of a bamboo skewer into each piece so that it has a handle.

STEP 1   STEP 2

3. Wrap each banana half in a piece of aluminum foil and place in the freezer until frozen solid, 4 to 6 hours or overnight.

4. Place the cream in a small saucepan and bring to a gentle simmer over medium heat. Remove from the heat.

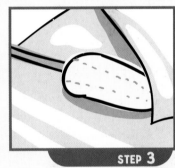

STEP 3

5. Place the chocolate chips in a medium mixing bowl, then carefully pour the hot cream over the chips. Let the chocolate and cream sit undisturbed for a minute or two, then stir with a small spoon or rubber spatula until the mixture is blended and smooth and the chocolate is completely melted, about 2 minutes.

STEP 5

6. Place the toasted coconut in a small mixing bowl.

7. If using nuts, chop into small pieces and place in a small mixing bowl.

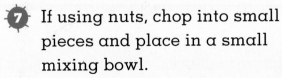

215

8 Remove the bananas from the freezer and unwrap.

9 Cover a small baking sheet with waxed paper or aluminum foil.

10 Holding the stick or skewer, dip one banana half in the melted chocolate and cream until completely coated.

11 Sprinkle the coated banana with about 1 tablespoon of either the toasted coconut or the chopped peanuts.

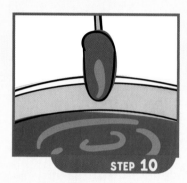

STEP 10

STEP 11

12 Set the banana on the covered baking sheet and repeat with the remaining bananas and coatings.

STEP 12

13 Serve immediately or cover tightly and return the bananas to the freezer until ready to serve.

SERIOUSLY CHOCOLATY CHEESECAKE

Yield

1 CHEESECAKE,
SERVING ABOUT 12

Ingredients

CRUST

½ CUP GRAHAM CRACKER CRUMBS

¾ CUP FINELY GROUND OREO
COOKIES (CHOCOLATE COOKIE
PART ONLY, NO WHITE FILLING)

4 TABLESPOONS (½ STICK)
UNSALTED BUTTER, MELTED

2 TABLESPOONS SUGAR

FILLING

6 OUNCES SEMISWEET CHOCOLATE

2½ POUNDS CREAM CHEESE,
SOFTENED

1½ CUPS SUGAR

1 TEASPOON VANILLA EXTRACT

1 TABLESPOON UNSWEETENED
COCOA POWDER

4 LARGE EGGS

½ CUP SOUR CREAM

1 (1½-OUNCE) MILK CHOCOLATE
BAR

Tools

MEASURING CUPS AND SPOONS,
LARGE MIXING BOWL, FORK,
9-INCH SPRINGFORM PAN, OVEN
MITTS OR POT HOLDERS,
MICROWAVE-PROOF BOWL,
PLASTIC WRAP, RUBBER SPATULA
OR LARGE SPOON, LARGE METAL
MIXING BOWL, ELECTRIC MIXER,
SIFTER, WIRE RACK, GRATER,
SHARP THIN KNIFE, PLASTIC WRAP

Mmmm . . . if you like chocolate as much as I like chocolate, then help yourself to a piece of this! It has all the usual goodness of a regular cheesecake, plus a rich, chocolaty flavor, an Oreo-cookie crust for a nice crunch, and then a grated Hershey's bar on top—oh, man, it's the best! This cheesecake makes an impressive dessert for special occasions, and because it's so rich, it can feed a crowd. Try making it a day in advance—it'll be easier to slice and serve once it's been refrigerated and is thoroughly chilled.

Directions

CAUTION
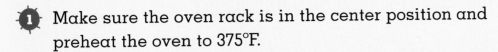

Be careful not to touch the hot pan when you add the grated chocolate to the hot cake!

CRUST

1 Make sure the oven rack is in the center position and preheat the oven to 375°F.

2 In a large mixing bowl, combine all the crust ingredients with a fork and mix until well combined.

3 Press the cookie mixture into the bottom of a 9-inch springform pan.

STEP 3

4 Bake the crust until fragrant and just set, about 8 to 10 minutes.

5 Using oven mitts or pot holders, remove from the oven and cool for at least 15 minutes before adding the filling.

6 Lower the oven temperature to 350°F.

FILLING

1 Place semisweet chocolate in a microwave-proof glass bowl or measuring cup and cover it with plastic wrap. Microwave the chocolate on high power for 30 seconds; then stir it with a spoon or rubber spatula. Continue to microwave the chocolate on high, stopping to stir every 30 seconds, until it is completely melted and smooth. (If you don't have a microwave, you can use the double-boiler method for melting chocolate on page 26.) Set aside.

2 Place the cream cheese, sugar, and vanilla extract in a large metal bowl and, using an electric mixer, beat until creamy and smooth, about 4 minutes. Turn the mixer off and scrape down the sides of the bowl with a rubber spatula (see page 24).

STEP 2

It's important not to add hot melted chocolate to the raw eggs, or you'll cook them!

3 Sift the cocoa powder into the cream cheese mixture and beat to incorporate. Turn the mixer off.

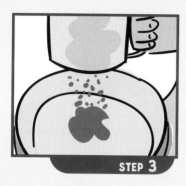

STEP 3

4 Crack and add the eggs one at a time, beating well after each addition. Be sure to turn the mixer off before you add each egg. Add the sour cream and melted chocolate and beat until smooth.

5 Using a rubber spatula, transfer the batter to the prepared pan with the baked crust.

STEP 4

STEP 5

6 Bake at 350°F until the cake rises and puffs and the center is just set and still slightly wiggly, about 1 hour and 10 minutes.

7 Using oven mitts or pot holders, remove from the oven and place on a wire rack to cool.

8 Grate the chocolate bar and sprinkle the shavings over the top of the cheesecake while it's still hot.

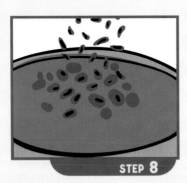

STEP **8**

9 Let the cheesecake cool for 1 hour.

10 Cover the cheesecake with plastic wrap and refrigerate at least 4 hours or overnight before serving.

11 When you're ready to serve the cheesecake, gently run a thin sharp knife around the inside edge of the springform pan to loosen the cake's sides, then unhook and carefully remove the outer ring of the pan. Slice and serve.

STEP **11**

Kick up your cheesecake by topping it with some fresh Whipped Cream (page 235).

APPLE-OF-MY-EYE CRISP

Yield
6 TO 8 SERVINGS

Ingredients
1 TABLESPOON PLUS
4 TABLESPOONS
(½ STICK) COLD
UNSALTED BUTTER CUT
INTO ½-INCH PIECES

½ CUP ALL-PURPOSE
FLOUR

¼ CUP LIGHT BROWN
SUGAR

¼ CUP PLUS ¾ CUP
GRANULATED SUGAR

¼ TEASPOON SALT

3 GRANNY SMITH
APPLES

3 GOLDEN DELICIOUS
APPLES

2 TEASPOONS FRESH
LEMON JUICE

1 TABLESPOON PLUS
1 TEASPOON
CORNSTARCH

1 TEASPOON
CINNAMON

Tools
MEASURING CUPS AND
SPOONS, 9 X 9-INCH
BAKING DISH, MEDIUM
MIXING BOWL, 2 FORKS
OR A PASTRY BLENDER,
VEGETABLE PEELER,
APPLE CORER, KNIFE,
CUTTING BOARD,
LARGE MIXING BOWL,
LARGE SPOON, OVEN
MITTS OR POT
HOLDERS

Here's a really old-fashioned, homey
dessert that takes me back to my childhood—a lot of
folks in New England like to make apple crisp in the
fall, when apples are at their best. I've used a
combination of tart and sweet apples here because I
think they're terrific together, but you could really
use any apples you like. The secret to a successful
crisp topping is to let it rest in the refrigerator while
you prepare the other ingredients. Oh, and if you
really want to kick this up notches unknown to
humankind, serve your apple crisp with a scoop or
two of vanilla ice cream
on top!

Directions

CAUTION

Be careful coring and slicing apples! Have an adult help you. And hey—be really careful taking the hot, bubbly crisp out of the oven.

1 Make sure the oven rack is in the center position and preheat the oven to 350°F.

2 Grease a 9 by 9-inch baking dish with 1 tablespoon of the butter. Set aside.

STEP **2**

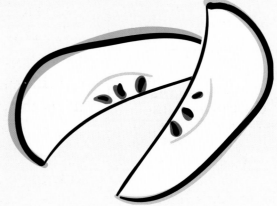

3 Place the flour, brown sugar, ¼ cup of the granulated sugar, and the salt in a medium mixing bowl.

4 Add the remaining 4 tablespoons of butter pieces and work them in with two forks, a pastry blender, or your fingers until the mixture resembles coarse crumbs. Refrigerate the crumb topping while preparing the other ingredients.

STEP **4**

STEP **5**

5 Peel and core the apples (page 20). Now cut one apple in half. Place one apple half flat on the cutting board and cut lengthwise into 6 slices.

223

6 Place the slices in a large mixing bowl and use your hands or a wooden spoon to toss with the lemon juice.

7 Repeat with the remaining apples, tossing with lemon juice after each addition.

8 Add the remaining ¾ cup of granulated sugar, the cornstarch, and the cinnamon to the apples and stir well with a large spoon.

9 Pour the apples into the prepared baking dish and crumble the topping evenly over the mixture.

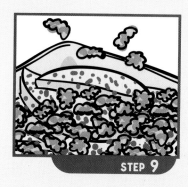
STEP 9

10 Bake until golden brown and bubbling, about 1 hour and 15 minutes.

11 Using oven mitts or pot holders, remove the dish from the oven and cool on a wire rack for 10 minutes before serving.

If you want to make a pie instead, just pour the apples into an (unbaked) store-bought or premade piecrust and proceed as directed above to make an apple crumb pie!

POKEY BROWNIES

Yield

TWENTY-FOUR 2-INCH-SQUARE BROWNIES

Ingredients

BROWNIES

1 TABLESPOON PLUS ¾ CUP (1½ STICKS) UNSALTED BUTTER

1 TABLESPOON PLUS ¾ CUP ALL-PURPOSE FLOUR, SIFTED

3 (1-OUNCE) SQUARES UNSWEETENED BAKING CHOCOLATE

1½ CUPS GRANULATED SUGAR

3 LARGE EGGS

1½ TEASPOONS VANILLA EXTRACT

1 CUP CHOPPED PECANS OR WALNUTS, LIGHTLY TOASTED (PAGE 233)

FUDGY TOPPING

½ CUP (1 STICK) UNSALTED BUTTER

¼ CUP UNSWEETENED COCOA POWDER

6 TABLESPOONS BUTTERMILK

1 POUND CONFECTIONERS' SUGAR

1 TEASPOON VANILLA EXTRACT

Tools

MEASURING CUPS AND SPOONS, 9 x 13 INCH BAKING PAN, LARGE GLASS MICROWAVE-PROOF MEASURING CUP OR MEDIUM GLASS BOWL, PLASTIC WRAP, LARGE MIXING BOWL, WIRE WHISK, TOOTHPICK, OVEN MITTS OR POT HOLDERS, WOODEN SPOON, RUBBER SPATULA, 2- TO 3-QUART SAUCEPAN, MEDIUM MIXING BOWL

You might look at the yield and think to yourself, "Self, I can eat a much bigger brownie than just a little two-inch one." But I tell you what, these are ultra-rich, and a little goes a long, long way! So while two inches doesn't seem big, I think you'll find it tough to eat a larger one. If you want, just make the basic brownie recipe without the icing. Pokey Brownies are pretty rich on their own and would make a terrific lunchbox treat.

BROWNIES

1 Make sure the oven rack is in the center position and preheat the oven to 350°F.

2 Grease a 9 by 13-inch baking pan with 1 tablespoon of the butter. Sprinkle 1 tablespoon of the flour into the pan and shake and swirl it to coat the sides and bottom evenly. Hold the pan over the sink or a trash can, then turn it upside down and lightly tap the bottom to release any extra flour. Set aside.

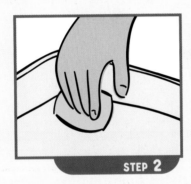

STEP **2**

3 Place the remaining 1½ sticks of butter and the chocolate in a large glass measuring cup or medium glass bowl, cover with plastic wrap, and microwave on high power for 1 minute. Remove from the microwave, uncover, and stir well.

4 Return the butter and chocolate mixture to the microwave and cook 30 to 60 seconds, or until the chocolate is melted. (If you don't have a microwave, combine the butter and chocolate in the top of a double boiler and follow the directions for the double-boiler method for melting chocolate on page 26.)

5. Pour the melted chocolate mixture into a large mixing bowl. Add the granulated sugar and whisk until smooth.

6. Add ¼ cup of the flour and whisk to combine. Crack and add 1 egg and whisk to combine. Alternate adding the remaining flour and eggs, whisking well after each addition.

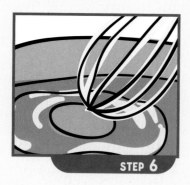
STEP 6

7. Stir in the vanilla and toasted nuts and mix well.

8. Pour the batter into the prepared pan. Holding the pan with both hands, give the bottom of the pan a quick rap against the countertop.

9. Bake until the brownies rise and a toothpick inserted into the center of the pan comes out clean, about 30 minutes (see page 27).

STEP 8

10. Using oven mitts or pot holders, remove the pan from the oven.

11. Use the handle of a wooden spoon to poke holes into the brownies every 1 to 2 inches.

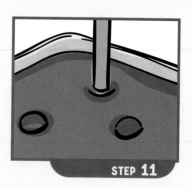
STEP 11

12 While it is still warm, pour the Fudgy Topping over the brownies and smooth it with a rubber spatula.

13 Let pan cool on a wire rack for at least 1 hour before serving brownies.

STEP 12

FUDGY TOPPING

1 Combine the butter, cocoa powder, and buttermilk in a medium saucepan and heat until the butter melts and the mixture just comes to a boil.

2 Remove from the heat and whisk until smooth.

3 Sift the confectioners' sugar into a medium mixing bowl.

4 Add the chocolate mixture and vanilla extract to the powdered sugar and whisk until smooth.

5 Pour over the brownies as directed above.

STEP 4

These brownies are really good warm, with a scoop of Real Vanilla-Bean Ice Cream (page 202) or Whipped Cream (page 235) on top!

CREAMY DREAMY ORANGE FREEZE

This super-refreshing dessert drink is easy to make and is a great breakfast treat, too. Try one next time you're in the mood for something to quench your thirst as well as satisfy your sweet tooth!

Yield

3 GENEROUS CUPS, SERVING ABOUT 4

Ingredients

2 CUPS ORANGE JUICE

1 CUP ICE CUBES

⅓ CUP NONFAT DRY MILK

¼ CUP HONEY

Tools

MEASURING CUPS, BLENDER

Directions

Make sure the blender top is on tight before you turn it on!

1. Combine all the ingredients in a blender and process on high speed until smooth and frothy, about 45 seconds.

2. Pour into glasses and serve.

STEP 1

Try adding a little pineapple juice or coconut milk to really kick this up a notch!

SIMPLE SYRUP

Once you get used to making your own Simple Syrup, you'll find that it makes cooking lots of different things much easier. We use it to make our Fresh-and-Fruity Freeze Pops (page 208), but you also can use it to make easy homemade lemonade. Go ahead and make a full (or half) recipe of Simple Syrup and store it in the refrigerator, where it'll keep for a couple of months. That way, when you want to whip up a sweet drink or frozen treat, you'll be ready to go and won't have to wait for the syrup to cool.

Directions

 **CAUTION**

Yield
2 ¼ CUPS

Ingredients
1 ½ CUPS SUGAR
1 ½ CUPS WATER

Tools
MEASURING CUPS,
3-QUART HEAVY
SAUCEPAN, STURDY
AIRTIGHT CONTAINER

1 Combine the sugar and water in a medium, heavy saucepan.

2 Bring to a boil without stirring.

3 Remove the pan from the heat and let it cool.

4 Pour the syrup into an airtight container and place in the refrigerator to cool completely (about 2 hours) before using.

5 Use as needed.

TOASTING THINGS

Many recipes call for toasted things, such as nuts or coconut and sometimes bread crumbs or croutons. This is pretty easy to do—just make sure you keep a close eye on whatever you're toasting because some foods toast quicker than others! You'll need either a toaster oven for small amounts or an oven for larger amounts, as well as a baking sheet large enough to hold whatever you're toasting in one even layer. Look below for instructions on toasting nuts and coconut—we use both in this book. If you want to try to toast other foods, just remember what I said about that timing thing! And hey— always toast in a not-too-hot oven, say 300°F to 350°F.

Ingredients

SWEETENED FLAKED COCONUT OR NUTS OF CHOICE

Tools

BAKING SHEET, OVEN MITTS OR POT HOLDERS, WIRE RACK

Directions

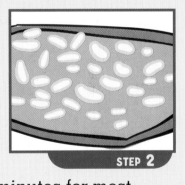

Be very careful taking the baking sheet out of the oven!

STEP 2

1 Make sure the oven rack is in the center position and preheat the oven to 350°F.

2 Spread the desired amount of coconut or nuts on a baking sheet and make sure they are spread evenly in one single layer. Use whole nuts or halves and chop after toasting if needed. Bake in the oven until just golden and very fragrant, 5 minutes for coconut and 8 to 10 minutes for most nuts.

3 Using oven mitts or pot holders, carefully remove the baking sheet from the oven and transfer to a wire rack to cool.

4 Use as desired or store in an airtight container, preferably in a cool location. Nuts will keep up to 2 weeks after toasting. Coconut usually gets less crispy after a day or two.

Whole nuts are best for toasting, though halves are okay, too. If the pieces are too small, this timing will be wrong and the nuts can easily burn.

233

Baby Bam

Here's something to season your foods, the way the grown-ups do with Emeril's Original Essence. Give it another dimension by sprinkling it into everything, from soups and sauces to pizza and hamburger patties. You fearless bammers out there can kick this up a notch by adding cayenne (I'd start with about ¼ teaspoon, and then take it from there).

Directions

Yield
ABOUT ¾ CUP

Ingredients
3 TABLESPOONS PAPRIKA

2 TABLESPOONS SALT

2 TABLESPOONS DRIED PARSLEY

2 TEASPOONS ONION POWDER

2 TEASPOONS GARLIC POWDER

1 TEASPOON GROUND BLACK PEPPER

1 TEASPOON DRIED OREGANO

1 TEASPOON DRIED BASIL

1 TEASPOON DRIED THYME

½ TEASPOON CELERY SALT

Tools
MEASURING SPOONS, MIXING BOWL, WOODEN SPOON, AIRTIGHT CONTAINER

1. Place all the ingredients in a mixing bowl.

2. Stir well to combine, using a wooden spoon.

3. Store in an airtight container for up to 3 months.

WHIPPED CREAM

Easy to make and so delicious, a dollop of whipped cream kicks just about any dessert into another dimension!

Directions

CAUTION

Yield

2 CUPS

Ingredients

1 CUP HEAVY CREAM, WELL CHILLED

2 TABLESPOONS CONFECTIONERS' SUGAR

¾ TEASPOON VANILLA EXTRACT

Tools

MEASURING CUPS AND SPOONS, MEDIUM MIXING BOWL, ELECTRIC MIXER (HANDHELD OR STANDING), PLASTIC WRAP (OPTIONAL)

1. Place the mixing bowl in the freezer or refrigerator about 15 minutes, or until it's well chilled.

2. Combine the heavy cream, powdered sugar, and vanilla extract in the mixing bowl.

3. With the electric mixer on low speed, begin beating the cream, gradually increasing the speed to high as the cream thickens. (Do this slowly, or the cream will splatter all over!)

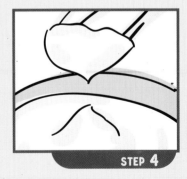

STEP 3

4. Beat until the cream forms soft peaks (page 24). Test to see if it is ready by turning off the mixer and lifting the beaters out of the cream—if the cream makes soft peaks that topple over slightly, then it's done. Be careful not to overwhip, or the cream will separate and begin to taste like butter.

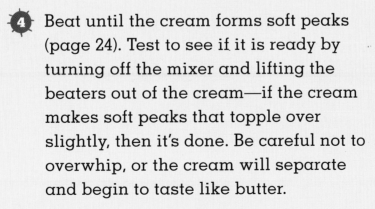

STEP 4

5. Serve immediately or cover with plastic wrap and refrigerate for up to 2 hours.

APPENDIX

EMERIL'S RESTAURANT GUIDE

EMERIL'S RESTAURANT
800 Tchoupitoulas Street
New Orleans, LA 70130
(504) 528–9393

NOLA RESTAURANT
534 Rue St. Louis
New Orleans, LA 70130
(504) 522–6652

EMERIL'S DELMONICO RESTAURANT AND BAR
1300 St. Charles Avenue
New Orleans, LA 70130
(504) 525–4937

EMERIL'S NEW ORLEANS FISH HOUSE
at the MGM Grand Hotel & Casino
3799 Las Vegas Boulevard South
Las Vegas, NV 89109
(702) 891–7374

DELMONICO STEAKHOUSE
at the Venetian Resort Hotel Casino
3355 Las Vegas Boulevard South
Las Vegas, NV 89109
(702) 414–3737

EMERIL'S RESTAURANT ORLANDO
at Universal Studios Escape
6000 Universal Boulevard
Universal Studios CityWalk
Orlando, FL 32819
(407) 224–2424

WEBSITE GUIDE

CHEF EMERIL LAGASSE
www.emerils.com

The official website for everything Emeril. Here you will find listings for all his restaurants, shows, and merchandise as well as in-depth background and insight into Emeril's culinary world, plus a monthly on-line magazine and recipes. Bam!

ALL-CLAD COOKWARE
www.emerilware.com

The cookware that Chef Emeril believes in. Here you will find the entire selection of Emerilware by All-Clad—from skillets to saute pans.

B&G FOODS
www.bgfoods.com

If you want to kick up your kitchen a notch, look for Emeril's Original spice blends, salad dressings, marinades, hot sauces, and pasta sauces. Created by Chef Emeril Lagasse himself and distributed by B&G Foods, Inc.

FOOD NETWORK
www.foodtv.com

Log on to the Food Network's site for all recipes and scheduling information for *Emeril Live* and *Essence of Emeril*, as well as ticket information for *Emeril Live*.

HARPERCOLLINS
www.harpercollins.com

This informative site offers background and chapter excerpts on all of Chef Emeril Lagasse's best-selling cookbooks.

INDEX